Praise for asha bandele and
THE PRISONER'S WIFE

"In lyrical, flowing prose, columnist and performance poet bandele presents piercing portraits of herself, the man she loves, and a prison system designed to stifle all sensibility. Mesmerizing and disconcerting. Offering insights into why caged birds sing."
— *Kirkus Reviews* (starred review)

"asha bandele tells the story of a love that flourishes in the constricted space between freedom and captivity. Ironically, the captive whom she loves helps her to extricate herself from her own emotional prison."
—Angela Y. Davis

"Echoes Edwidge Danticat's *Farming of the Bones* in the urgency in which it reminds us of the possibility of love even amidst ruins. This is a terrifying, heartbreaking, and, ultimately, important book. . . . *THE PRISONER'S WIFE* can be our talisman, our healing potion, how we keep breathing—as they lock up numbers beyond comprehension, [this book] reminds us that we can survive, even if it is only two at a time."
—Junot Diaz

"With an exquisite narrative, asha bandele captures your imagination as she gifts the reader with an extraordinary story of human destiny."
—*African Sun Times*

"Powerful, poignant . . . soul-shaking. . . . *THE PRISONER'S WIFE* is a cry of love in a cold, bleak wilderness and, as such, it underscores and defines our basic humanity, and our abiding strength to endure."
—Bob Shacochis

Also by asha bandele

Absence in the Palms of My Hands and Other Poems

The Prisoner's Wife

a memoir

asha bandele

WASHINGTON SQUARE PRESS
PUBLISHED BY POCKET BOOKS

New York   London   Toronto   Sydney   Singapore

WSP

A Washington Square Press Publication of
POCKET BOOKS, a division of Simon & Schuster Inc.
1230 Avenue of the Americas, New York, NY 10020

Copyright © 1999 by asha bandele

Originally published in hardcover in 1999 by Scribner

Library of Congress Cataloging-in-Publication Data

bandele, asha.
    The prisoner's wife : a memoir / asha bandele.
      p. cm.
    Originally published: New York : Scribner, c1999.
    ISBN 0-671-02148-6
    1. bandele, asha—Marriage. 2. Poets, American—
20th century—Biography. 3. Prisoners' spouses—United
States—Biography. 4. Married people—United States—
Biography. 5. Afro-American women poets—Biography. I. Title.

PS3552.A47527 Z47 2000
811'.54—dc21
[B]   00-036312

First Washington Square Press trade paperback printing August 2000

10 9 8 7 6 5 4 3

Cover design by Brigid Pearson
Front cover photo by John Sann

Printed in the U.S.A.

For Rashid
over and over and over

. . . if i know anything at all,
it's that a wall is just a wall
and nothing more at all.
it can be broken down.
—assata shakur

Acknowledgments

There's no way that a book like this cannot be considered a collaborative effort. Trying to tell a very personal story while you're still in the midst of the drama requires a particular and consistent kind of support. It's the kind that comes at four in the afternoon and four in the morning. It's the kind that comes even when you think you don't need it. It pays your little attitude no attention and just walks right in, grabs you and holds you, until you laugh or cry or talk. Or write. You begin to write and when that happens, that release, you feel as close to freedom as this life will ever allow. There were so many people who, in a myriad of ways, gave me that gift. And they gave it to me again and again. I swear I don't know how to begin to thank them, but I do know I must at least call their names, say publicly that the best that this book has to offer is surely a reflection of their love and humanity.

First of all to my parents, who have resigned themselves to simply loving their difficult and strange daughter. Thank you. To my sister, who listens and listens, and who always works to understand, and to T'Kalla, Asale Ajani, Christa Bell, Robin Templeton, and Laila Jenkins, who took my relationship seriously from the very beginning, and who read and critiqued the manuscript along the way. Thank you. To the membership of the New Afrikan Independence Movement—with a particular affection for the Brooklyn Chapter of Malcolm X Grassroots Movement—for vision, for strength, for an end goal, asante sana.

To Khadijah Diouf, Monifa Akinwole, Vera Beatty, Tanaquil Jones, Kim Wade, Talibah Nomakhosi, Christian Fabian, Letta Neely, Reggie Richardon, Michele Brown, Dagmar Schnau,

Ahmed Obafemi, Jalil Muntaquin, Sekou Odinga, Mutulu Shakur, Lumumba Bandele, Safiya Bandele, and especially to Dr. Errol Henderson for never letting me backslide into mediocrity, asante sana.

To Bob Shacochis, who suggested once that perhaps living well was not the best revenge, and that writing well was. If this book in some way rises to the occasion, it is in no small part due to the attention you paid to it. Thank you. To Meri Danquah who believed in my work "just based on your spirit," she said, and then introduced me to the most incredible and brilliant agent in the whole world: Victoria Sanders. And Victoria, who always makes me feel like I'm the most important, the most talented. Should we even speculate on what kind of basketcase would I have been without you?

Writers always seem to have countless war stories about slash-and-burn editors with whom they can never find peace. While I don't want to invalidate their experiences, I do want to throw mine into the discussion as well. I want to say that I wish they'd worked with my editor, Gillian Blake, who saw fifty pages of disconnected writing, and said, here: this is the needle and this is the thread. All you have to do is take it one stitch at a time. Thank you.

And to the incredible and complex people of Brooklyn, New York, from East Flatbush to Bed-Stuy, from Fort Greene to Crown Heights: for everything we are and everything we are not, for all the swagger and strength, the inspiration and beauty and truth, for providing me with a home into which I can one day welcome my husband.

And at last, to the women I ride the vans with, the ones with whom I've traded stories and laughter while we've waited and waited on this side of the wall. May the time pass quickly. May the hurt be mitigated by the love.

The Prisoner's Wife

this is a love story

*t*his is a love story like every love story I had always known, like no love story I could ever have imagined. It's everything beautiful—bright colors, candle-scented rooms, orange silk, and lavender amethyst. It's everything grotesque, disfigured. It's long twisting wounds, open and unhealed, nerves pricked raw, exposed.

This is a love story, awake and alive. It's a breathing document, a living witness. It's human possibility, hope, and connection. It's a gathering of Spirit, the claiming of dreams. It's an Alvin Ailey dance, a *rainbow roun' mah shoulder.* It's a freedom song, a 12-string guitar, a Delta blues song. This story is a reprieve.

This is a love story, threadbare and used up, yet sometimes fat, weighty, stretched out of shape. It's polyester, this story, man-made, trying to be pretty, not quite making it. This is a story desperate to hold itself together. This is a story with patches in the knees.

This is a love story, my love story and thousands of other women's love story. It's a story that's known, documented, photographed, videotaped, audiotaped, filed, photocopied, watched over, studied, caricatured, questioned, researched, and noted.

This is a love story. It's the one we keep close, sheltering it from judgment. It's lovers denied at family dinners and at office parties. It's secret glances at Polaroid pictures. It's whispered names. This is a story hidden within midnight bus rides and 5:00 A.M. van rides, behind metal detectors, electronic doors, and steel slamming against steel.

This is a love story, the one not generally discussed in polite or even public conversation. But if there's one thing that I do know about myself, it's that I know I hate secrets, that secrets mean shame, and that I am not now, nor will I ever be, ashamed that I am a woman who has loved someone, and that someone has loved me.

And even though so many people have asked me if I have lost my mind, if I am lonely, or desperate. Even though so many people have wondered if I was having a crisis, or determined that I was just going through a phase, I will continue loving the man I am loving. I will love him even though he's got an ugly past, skeletons, and sorrow. Even though he doesn't have a great job or position or power, and even though he's a prisoner at a maximum-security correctional facility, which my husband, Rashid, is, I will continue loving him.

And this is our story.

∾

The first time I ever went into a prison, it was for a class I was taking on the relationship between Black people and incarceration in the United States. Months later, long after final exams had been taken and grades received, my former professor called me and asked if I would come with him and a few other people to a place called Eastern Correctional Facility in upstate New York. It was just about eighty miles from Brooklyn, where I lived. He wanted me, he said, to participate in a Black History Month program.

Don't you write poems? he asked.

You could read your poetry, he said.

I agreed and we all went to do the program, and this was how we met, Rashid and I, convict and student, gangster and poet, resident host and visiting performer.

∾

Rashid is fine as hell, which I tried not to but couldn't help noticing the very first time I saw him. He looks like this beautifully symmetrical collaboration between Africa and India. He isn't huge, not an overwhelming presence, contrary to the usual celluloid interpretation of Black prisoners. Rashid is 5'7", with a brave smile and bright eyes. He is, I remember thinking this then, just the right size, and I could look directly at him, nearly eye to eye. His voice, which was never loud, told a story of a transplanted Afro-Caribbean.

Where are you from? I wanted to know.

The Boogie Down, he responded, meaning the South Bronx.

And before?

Oh, oh, he said, understanding my question. *Guyana. South America. It's the most beautiful place in the world. That's a hell of a thing in one life, huh? To have seen the most beautiful place in the world and the most horrible place. And I'm not even thirty yet!*

After that, a number of other men came over to me to tell me how much they enjoyed my performance, and would I be willing to read their work, when was I coming back up, could they write to me to discuss poetry, did I know I reminded them of this sister they used to know back in the day? In the midst of these questions, Rashid left me. I watched him as he walked across the huge auditorium where the program was being held. He weaved easily through the nearly one hundred men gathered there, through the orange chairs, across the stage, the back of it, and found another guest to talk to, a poet like me. A very talented poet, I should say, and a very attractive one. I waited for him to come back over to me. I tried to will him to come back over to me, but finally I was left there annoyed because Rashid did not return until it was time to say good-bye.

After we were in love, Rashid would tell me that it was me, my fault, that I was hard to approach. He told me that while I was an animated and exciting performer, offstage I was quiet, withdrawn, cool and distant.

Besides, he admits now, through a series of childlike giggles, *every dude knows when you* really *want to talk to a sister, you don't step to her directly. You step to her friend, and that's what I did. I talked to that other sister, the poet who performed before you, because that way I knew I'd get your attention. I mean, what I'd look like trying to talk to you when all of them other dudes were running they game on you? You know what I'm saying?*

Rashid is *so* pleased with himself as he tells me this story *five* years after our first encounter. After all, in the moment of his confession, we are in a visiting room, and I lie, as fitted as possible, in the crook of his arms. And in that moment, despite every hurting and hell I have had to endure to love this man, there is no other place that I would rather be.

≈

When we began, I was twenty-five, a student and organizer, a wife on the verge of divorce from my first husband, a poet full of secrets and sadness, an emerging woman hampered by insecurities and anger, a human being fighting off loneliness while craving solitude, needing an open love, long honest discussions, a quiet touching at my core.

When we began, he was twenty-nine, inmate number 83*****, a convicted killer doing twenty years with life on the back, a model prisoner, a program coordinator, the father of a nine-year-old boy he had never been able to raise, a lawyer without a law degree, a devoted Muslim, a man on the verge of divorce from his first wife, a human being fighting off loneliness while craving solitude, needing an open love, long honest discussions, a quiet touching at his core.

We were exactly the same and we were completely different.

We were never meant to be together.

We were always meant to save each other.

home

When I look back at us now, the group of students who traipsed up into the prisons all those years ago to participate in the various programs, I always remember how we felt like Rashid was home from the very beginning. There was something about him, his warmth, his lack of an agenda that made it appear that there was no division, no difference between him and us, his world and ours.

Speaking at a prison can be a very overwhelming experience. Prisoners, already isolated, often make an intensely appreciative audience, and if you say things which in any way reflect their thinking, you can really get bombarded by requests at the close of a presentation. Folks are seeking pen pals, people to review their poetry and writings, any kind of connection to "the street." And as much as we may have wanted to, it was simply impossible for one or two or four people to serve that kind of mass need. But at such young ages, with virtually no primer before going into the facility, we didn't have any idea how to respond to what usually amounted to a hundred different requests for a hundred different things from a hundred different people.

This was why Rashid stood out, not just with me, but with all of us. He never asked us for anything. He just talked and talked with us. We talked about the struggle for equal education, world politics, social justice. We talked as though we were painters, using words like fluid strokes across the broad canvas which was our collective imagination. And the more we visited, the more we talked. And sometimes we agreed on things, and sometimes we disagreed on things, but it never got heated, ugly, or nasty. We were talking like we wanted to learn something. We were talking like we wanted to heal.

We were talking as though we believed our talking could change things, restore balance, make somebody free. It was unifying talk. And Rashid knew it, we all knew it. Rashid knew, as we knew, that he had become our friend, a member of our little clique, and this is what made it so difficult finally, when we would, at the end of a program, walk out of the prison without him. It seemed that if we meant anything we said in those long political discussions, there would just be no way we could have gone, leaving him behind then. Leaving him behind now.

వ

When people have asked me how could I have fallen in love with a man who was convicted of murder, where I begin is as a student who was volunteering time and hoping that my poems and willingness to talk would somehow change someone for the better. Then I tell about the man who would become my husband, how his spirit engaged me, engaged every one of us, and how by the openness of his spirit, it was I who would change.

Back then, during those early days of friendship, I learned something about taking in different points of view, listening carefully, reserving judgment, and not having to win an argument for winning's sake. I learned by watching Rashid, who always spoke in turn, and who spoke deliberately, and who admitted being wrong if he'd been shown to be wrong.

Prison, he told me one day, *will teach a man to be polite.*

The tension's so high here, you don't want to add to it by not say-

ing "excuse me" if it's right to say "excuse me." And that's good. I wasn't always like that. I used to be so arrogant.

I've explained to people that I didn't, despite what it would seem, fall in love with a killer. I fell in love with a man who wanted to become his own more perfect creation, a man committed to the transformation of himself, of the world. And the world he imagined was like the world I imagined. It was a place that was just and fair and safe and livable. We could meet there, in that place. We could meet there as creators. We could meet there as equals.

He valued my opinions! I have said this to friends.

Can you imagine such a man? He wants to consult with me about everything. Everything! He takes my advice, I have said to whoever would listen.

When I talked about things Rashid had never heard of, he took notes. *But it's more than this,* I've said, trying to get in every point I could while they were still paying attention.

He respects me enough to argue with me, I told my girlfriend one afternoon.

I never used to able to imagine that, I said to her. To be engaged in a debate, and I didn't mean the way men usually argue with women in that, *Okay, dear, whatever you say* kind of way. No! I meant the way men argue with men, as though the other person was a worthy opponent. Rashid listened to me and he challenged me. That's who I fell in love with, I said over and over. A man who believed I was a woman who was worth it.

Sometimes when I've told people these things, they say they just can't see it. *Where's the ugly stuff?* I've been asked over and over. And I've told them yes, it was true, that there were some women for whom ugliness and hurt was the texture of their story, but it simply was not the picture that I had to draw.

asha, some have argued, *girl, you have blinders on. He might be great now, but who is he going to be when he comes home?*

I don't know, I respond. *Who will I be?*

Rashid could come home and be horrible to you, I've been warned.

Yes, I tell them. *Of course that's true. But Rashid could also come home and be wonderful to me. None of us know tomorrow, only this moment, now, this time, already recorded in history.*

And this moment when I am kissed, nurtured, rocked, and then set at ease by the love I have been given, this moment is the only real thing I know. That, and also this one other thing: that there are so many people who are lonely, without love and without passion in their lives, that I know that what I have, as difficult as it may be, is the most precious of all gifts.

And I couldn't just give it up without a fight, this rare, this desired thing, this thing which is life-sustaining. Could I? Could they, I ask? I want to know this. Could they reject the greatest love they've ever known just because it came from the worst place they've ever known?

∾

Still I am aware that all things happen in a context, and so, Rashid's many charms notwithstanding, it is also true that there was this confluence of events in my life, and together they probably assisted in making him so significant to me.

The world is so magnificent, the way it keeps rebirthing itself to you, if you're amenable. And if you're amenable, the way the world comes will be exciting, new each time, in different colors, different shapes.

For me, a brand-new world was born when I became a student at the City University of New York. I majored in political science and Black studies, not realizing that within each classroom I would find pieces of myself, scattered pieces of Black female me just waiting to be scooped up and reattached.

For the first time in my life, a life which had been dominated by white history, white cultures, white literature, white music, white sensibilities, a life where Black was a metaphor for less than, I was reading books with characters and experiences that I understood. I was finally offered a history that went beyond slavery to include that which was Black and successful, Black and intelligent, Black and encouraging.

Learning this left me with a range of emotions I think common to any conquered people. The greatest, the most profound one I had, was love, at last for myself, as a Black woman, a woman who indeed had a place in history, if not in high school textbooks. For the first time in my entire academic history, I was studying the literature of Black people: James Baldwin and Zora Neale Hurston, Buchi Emecheta and Chinua Achebe.

I learned that there was more to my ancestry than slavery and the Civil Rights movement, which during my grammar and high school years were the only contexts in which I'd heard Black people being discussed. I could, at that pivotal juncture in my academic career, study Malcolm X, not as an extra-credit project, but as an extraordinary international political figure who had moved from prison to the Bandung Conference to the Organization of AfroAmerican Unity. I am embarrassed to admit this but I know it has to be said. For the first time in my life, I was truly and completely proud to be Black. I had never felt that before. Not once. Not all the way.

But at the same time that I was virtually falling in love with my history and culture, I was also feeling a huge sense of grief over what had been done to my people, what had been lost, who had been murdered. There was, certainly, a rage, a nearly unmitigated rage, at the people who made the policies and laws and institutions which could only be called evil.

I tell you this so that you understand how easy it was in those days to determine who was friend and who was enemy. Later, as I matured, took in more and more information, nothing stayed simple and clear. But it was, then, literally and figuratively, a black-and-white situation. And it was through this lens that I first saw not only Rashid, but all prisoners.

Back then I saw all prisoners as victims. I told Rashid this.

Yes, well, a lot of us also think like that in the beginning, he said to me.

And some people really are, straight-up, victims. At first we say we're all political prisoners because of the politics of the criminal justice system. And race is always an issue. But you know, as you get older, you want to take responsibility for all your life. Because if you live long enough, you do good things too. And I began to want to claim the good I had done. But if I was responsible for that, then I had to be responsible for the bad, too, right?

༺

Yet it wasn't only this emerging worldview which influenced my choices. There were indeed some tangible and devastating things which happened all at once, in the year just before I fell in love with Rashid. There were these departures. Suddenly everything in my life was shifting aside, seeking a fast exit, and I was just there, crouched on a curb, alone, unable to see across distances, unable to get perspective.

The initial blow came when I was put out of school for protesting against the steady tuition increases and budget cuts which were closing more and more students out of an education. We had rallied, marched, lobbied, and then occupied the administration building of our school. And it was for this final act that a few of us were brought up on internal charges, found guilty, and removed.

For two reasons, this was a bigger loss than I had anticipated. First of all, I was president of my student government, and therefore largely defined by school activities. But second, my own parents had been administrators at the university. And to be sure, they disagreed with the tuition increases and budget cuts as well, but more than anything, they wanted me to graduate. They said this to me then, and as much as I wanted to comply, I would in fact make them wait some five years before I paraded in black to the proud hum of *Pomp and Circumstance*.

Fourteen years before, when I was fifteen years old, I had walked a similar parade to the same song down the aisle of my high school auditorium. There were many valleys, long drops down and down further between those two days, and in all that time, despite my often hostile outward behavior, what had always been of greatest important to me is what was of greatest importance to many children.

I wanted desperately to please my parents, to make them proud. My parents, I knew, had made incredible sacrifices for my sister and me, to have a nice home, to go to good schools, to be exposed to the arts. We were middle-class but never rich by any stretch of the imagination. Whatever we had, my sister and I, came as a result of the long, often arduous hours my parents put in at their respective jobs.

And they were jobs that were not necessarily dream jobs— not my parents in jobs that nurture your soul. My mother and father worked so that my sister and I could have that sort of option, to work in any field we wanted. It would be a long time before I was old enough to understand this, to see my sister and myself as the major works of my parents' lives, my sister and myself as their legacies. And only then would my studies become an urgent matter. In my generation, it seems, most of us struggle for position and status. But my parents, their struggle was for us, their children, and I believed I owed them.

I knew I had been a very difficult teenager, more sullen, a worse student than the other young people my parents knew. My various misdeeds, the hanging out, the skipping school, the drugs, the drinking, they had stolen away the chance for my parents to be proud as I pondered which Ivy League school I would attend; in fact I only initially made it into college because of people my mother had known. And then just as I had settled down some four years later, just as I transferred into the City University and began making all A's, this: the protests, the charges, and finally, the suspension.

In a sense, losing my student status in the last half of my senior year meant losing something of my parents. I felt a bit like they had given up on me. I was, after all, in my twenties now. What more could they do?

≈

Against the disastrous backdrop of being put out of school, my precariously situated marriage toppled. I was twenty-three and two years married.

It was not that we didn't love each other, my first husband and I. It was that love was all we had. And we needed so much more. All couples do. We needed common passions and interests and goals. We needed to enjoy speaking with each other. We needed, then, some great omniscient who could have explained him to me, me to him.

What we had, instead, was silence. And in the face of that hard, that unfriendly quiet, my husband ran to work and stayed there for sometimes twelve, thirteen hours a day. I ran to school and did the same. By the time we'd come home, what else was there to do but sleep?

And we did, we slept. We slept fitfully, angrily, accusingly, but most of all, we slept singularly. We slept until there was nothing left to do except crawl out of bed, separately, and go on out into those two distinct worlds we had created for ourselves, his on one side of the universe, mine on the other.

And again my parents, with their happy, healthy, four-decade long marriage, my parents did not agree with or understand, how, after only two years, it could all fall apart. Everything had been so carefully constructed. I had, all of us had, listened to the experts, and tried to follow suit.

My first husband and I began life with an expensive, formal June wedding. I wore a white gown and veil. My father walked me down the aisle, and danced the first dance with me. We had joint bank accounts and credit cards. My husband said I didn't have to work, just go to school. I went to school. I cooked and cleaned. We had dinner parties. But in the end none of it worked because while we had the administrative part of it down, we were missing the creative. It didn't work because in the end, there were no words, no ongoing dialogues, no private jokes between us. And for many people, the absence of language is not enough reason to end a marriage. But for me it was the primary reason to do it. I know this now. I didn't know it then and this is why I could not run home to her, to my mother, who had, I'm sure, worked through and across silences to sustain her partnership with my father.

The bottom line was this: I wasn't running for my life from some kind of a monster, a batterer, a raging alcoholic. I was running from a man everybody loved, a man I loved. And this was why things got blamed on me. I had destabilized my own life, and then had the audacity to want sympathy, a shoulder, a helping hand.

I couldn't stay in a school. I couldn't stay in a marriage. I didn't have a job. So where could I stay? Who could I love? What could I do? What goal *could* I meet?

In the middle of the night, these questions would bang in my head. They would bang, like thick lead pipes against the sides of my dreams, bang and bang until I awoke. Awoke in fits of fear, sadness, isolation.

≈

I wanted love in my life again. I wanted to be important to someone again. I wanted to be accepted by someone again. My parents' disappointment, and my husband's disinterest, those things pushed and pricked like a thousand tiny pins menacing the soles of my feet. Whenever I walked, the pain of their rejection, what I translated as their rejection, would contort me; I suspected I looked like a sideshow act. That, or else an obvious failure. And I didn't know how not to be these things, how not to appear freakish, how not to be an outcast in the eyes of my family, and yes, in the eyes of men. That's the way breakups always seemed to leave me, especially at first, feeling undesirable, unlovable, ugly.

It was then no one single thing, but this terrific twister of loss and need that carried me into loving Rashid. For a year or more, he had been consistently inviting me up to the prisons to be part of their various cultural heritage shows, and I had gone each time, bringing other young people with me. One summer afternoon, I brought two young men I knew with me to do hip-hop poetry. One of the young men, a brother with a beautiful, sharp, carved face, stepped up to the mike. His tiny dreds stood firm on top of his head and it seemed like he was looking at everyone in the audience all at once, me, the prisoners, the police, everyone. Then he said, and I will never forget this,

Feel the rage of my warrior's wrath, as I pave a path of resistance.
I want to put a head out. Now!

As soon as those words hit the air, the stage was surrounded by more police than I have ever seen at one time, before or since, in a prison.

All right! That's it! one of the police said, and we were told we were going to have to leave the facility for "attempting to start a riot."

Before we were shoved out, I gave Rashid my home phone number. If we were being put out, I thought, what will they do to Rashid since he invited us up here?

Call me, I told him. I closed his hand around the tiny scrap of paper I had scribbled my number on.

Call me if they give you any trouble because of this.

Weeks, eight, maybe nine, pass between that incident and the first time I would answer my phone and hear what has now become an urgent and familiar recording:

You have a collect call from . . . Rashid . . . an inmate at a correctional facility. If you wish to decline the call, hang up. To accept press three, now.

And I did it. I pressed three and every part of my life, how I think, how I love, how I set priorities, what I pray for, what I treasure, what angers me, what I appreciate, how I organize my time, my money, every little thing in my life, and every big thing, changed. And it changed before I had a chance to seek consultation or ask a question. It changed before I had a chance to pause or reconsider. Or run.

this is the way
you court a poet

*t*he weeks that lead up to our first visit are now a blur of breathy phone calls and intense, biweekly letters. I told my girlfriends, the ones who asked me, that Rashid managed to romance me completely through those initial exchanges. I told them that it was those letters that hooked me. I told them that no woman has ever gotten a love letter until they've gotten a love letter from a man in prison.

Unlike my friends who have lovers whose range of feeling, they said, orbited within these two spheres: anger and lust, Rashid sweated out his emotion. *Every bit of it,* I told them. *He doesn't hold back on me the way so many men do.* All of Rashid's concerns and fears meet the paper, absent machismo, with a particular urgency: *Baby, I called last night, where were you?* Or: *asha, I didn't wanna love you like this 'cause I'm afraid you'll leave too, but I can't help it . . . you're so goddamn sweet.* But most often he just said: *Mama, if I could just hold you right now, if I could just touch you . . .*

Rashid was not a beautiful writer, no singing metaphors, no high art. But he was expressive, honest, and clear. He was vulnerable and so spiritually generous. Rashid gave me something I never had. Until we became involved, I had never been romanced. Surprise gifts, gooey cards, sappy words had never been mine.

When I fell in love with Rashid, already I had been married and had also lived with boyfriends, but still I was sure that romance was for other girls, delicate girls, the girls who I knew all throughout high school who heard their names called out over the radio: *That's "Ebony Eyes" going out to Yvonne from Michael with all of his love, always and forever* . . .

At twenty-five when Rashid sent me my first love letter, he dedicated a song by Luther Vandross to me in it. Maybe another woman my age would have thought this gesture was corny or juvenile. I cried. I thought it was oxygen.

When Rashid wrote, he wrote about my eyes. He said they were sexy, intimate, bedroom eyes. He said they were dangerous eyes. At least dangerous for men, he said. No one had ever commented much on what my eyes looked like. Who sees your eyes when you're fourteen years old with *double D*-cup breasts? Or twenty-two, for that matter, who looks at your eyes?

The first time Rashid told me that he thought my eyes were one of my most beautiful features, I was insulted. I didn't know then that it was a compliment. I thought compliments could only be about legs, breasts, asses, and hips.

Let me tell you, that man courted me, all soft words and pure desire. No hidden agendas, no games, no emotional retardation, only reverence and passion from behind all of that stone and concrete, that steel and razor wire. It was out of a movie, an epic romance, the way Rashid loved, the way he wanted to be loved in return.

To this very day, his approach licks itself around my waist, tender, and without aggression. To this day, Rashid is unhurried, allowing me to direct the movement and pace, but always letting me know he is open, all the way, and ready for whatever I offer, whenever I offer it. No one, I am not exaggerating, no one had ever treated me like that, like a woman who ought to be handled with care.

I used to harass the mailman during those first few months. I used to stand there, staring over him as he dropped letters, bills, and magazines into other people's boxes, slowly making his way down to mine. I would sigh at him, dramatic and heavy. I would shift from one foot to the other, *real* heavy. When he did finally get to me, I would snatch that mail out of his hands and nearly knock him over as I pushed past him to race up the stairs to my apartment.

Once back home, I would throw, with disgust, all of my roommate's mail aside along with anything that came for me which was not clearly stamped *Eastern Correctional Facility.*

It was a ridiculous ritual.

I never even read Rashid's letters until hours later, when it was dark, long into the night. I wanted to be sure I wouldn't be interrupted by my roommate or the telephone. All these years later, I haven't changed this practice.

You have to understand, Rashid's letters are like dates. I have to get myself ready. I have to give them their proper space. Before I read his letters, I take a long, mango-scented bath. I burn white candles around the edge of the tub, and sandalwood incense, serenade my own self with Nina Simone songs (*Do I move you, are you willing*).

After, when I am dried and oiled and stretched out, when I have made a cup of vanilla tea, when I am dressed in something silk and loose, then I can invite Rashid in. *Come in,* I can say, and he does. And we sit for a while, speak softly and then rise, decide to go out, to breathe the night air together.

In those letters Rashid and I take long slow walks across the Brooklyn Bridge holding hands. Those letters, they are easy discussions over dinner. They're whispers on the slow, blue-light dance floor. They are 3:00 A.M. pillow talk. They are the embraces I crave, those letters. I dream by them, and they assure me that after an unsteady or else unforgiving night, morning comes. Morning always comes.

In the very beginning of our exchanges Rashid would also, in what I'm sure was an attempt to validate and provide context and history for our relationship, lift whole paragraphs out of *Soledad Brother.* And when he didn't lift words, he lifted arguments, until finally I complained. I told him that it didn't work for him to write as though he was George Jackson and I was Angela Davis. It was romantic, I told him, but we had a responsibility to be honest about ourselves. At this particular juncture in time, we didn't really have the skills to develop a theory that could liberate all Black people. One day. I could see it one day. But this day was just about us, which sounded so selfish, I cringed as I said it.

Still, if I was certain of anything, I was certain that we had to begin by learning how to love ourselves first, love ourselves fully first. If we could manage to do that, without codependence or control issues, we might really become useful to other Black people, I said. Useful to the world, I said.

discovery

Rashid and I gave ourselves up to each other, publicly, in monitored phone calls, in scrutinized letters, and finally on videotape in prison visiting rooms. The months of our courtship fell without discipline and formed these odd mountains of time; before we knew it we were involved, an item, a tiny team climbing, our eyes shut tight, never looking down or back. And although it took many, many tries over many, many years, we did do it. We did reach the top of the mountain and we named that summit trust. We named it love, unconditional, and this was how we were able to thoroughly and completely turn back the years to each of our beginnings.

In the eight years we have now been together, through hushed and sometimes hesitating voices, we have excavated all of our years, the years of our lives that had been ripped in the center, the years without days, the years greater than the sum of their parts. We have examined these years, whatever has been left of them. We have laid them out and we have labeled them, but sometimes, when we have grown very tired, we have set them aside. We have left them alone for long, long periods. But we have never abandoned our journey (ourselves). We have always come back, always. We have faced our years and all that they have been, and all that they have not been, and we have tried, this I know for certain, we have tried as hard as two people have ever tried anything, to make some sort of peace with them.

Long into our relationship, I would see that our sharing,

our examining of ourselves, with all of its fervor, was, in a
sense, a gift that the prison had given us. If strangers and even
enemies could read our every letter, listen in on our every
phone call, if they could witness our fights and our tears, if
they could watch as the snot came down my face when I
heaved, sobbed, and prayed for strength, what was there to
hide from the person whom I loved?

But as incredible as our journey was and still is, it has also
been intensely isolated, which is why friends question me constantly. They have often wondered out loud if I rushed head-
long into some dangerous love affair, and I admit at first I had
these intermittent doubts, not about Rashid, but about
whether or not we could make a relationship something real,
something we could touch, something that would sustain us.

Initially, I did tell Rashid we would have to go slow, just
writing letters, just talking on the phone. A visit could come
later, I said. But even those doubts, when I think about them
now, I know they were really nothing more than background
noise, and we easily blocked them out with all of our need, our
nearly desperate willingness to love, and yes, even laughter, we
blocked them with laughter as well.

Over two months, in thirty-two letters, twenty-four phone
calls, and innumerable fantasies, we created ourselves, Rashid
and I, as a couple, and in our eyes, a man and woman as normal as the men and women I'd see each day, together, holding
hands, and taking for granted that very act, the holding of
hands.

For us, and I mean the us who lived, not split in half by law
and steel but the us from the letters and the fantasies, our
romance was the truth. Everything else was a lie. This is what
we believed then. And somehow, with so many of our dreams

chipped or cracked or else ruined forever, this is what we believe now, today, in this moment of writing.

In a sense, an emotional sense if not a physical sense, our beginning really could have been anyone's beginning, imbued as it was with the familiar sort of nervous energy that undermined the struggle to be funny, charming, endearing, and brilliant in each statement.

Of course, back then my life had not become some imperiled landscape, a city existing upon a faultline; I didn't know then how it would be, living with the daily threat that everything I knew could break into unsalvageable pieces in a few violent angry seconds. I didn't know then how I would be stalked by the fear that in just one prison uprising, in even just one disagreement with a guard, what small joy Rashid and I might have created could be destroyed. I didn't know then what it would mean to consciously hand over the control of happiness in my life. Not all of it. But so much of it. Too much of it, there, held tight in the unpredictable hands of prison life.

from the defense's files

*f*reedom, having the perfect love beside me, these things never seemed distant or impossible. Rather they were a tease, only barely out of my reach. If only I was granted one inch more we would be touching, Rashid and I, fingertip to fingertip. It made me obsessive, trying to figure out how to make my vision three-dimensional. It nearly swallowed me, the grasping and then missing, and then grasping once again. But I didn't lose hope. I just kept reaching, compulsive, like an addict. And Rashid, he fed this too, he was no innocent here.

How can I explain the way faith constructs itself within the narrow architecture of correctional institutions? They're not natural, these facilities, there's not ever enough space for a human being to live. And because of this, you have no choice, really. In order to survive, you must expand not only what you believe, but also how you go about believing it. You must expand it until you're nearly like a small child, accepting the implausible, the fantastic.

Rashid never believed that he would do all twenty years, which is the minimum time the state requires that he serves on his sentence. No one in prison ever thinks they're *really* going to take away all of that time from you, all of that life. He convinced me of this, that he would be home any minute. He convinced me because he was himself convinced.

Even when I was alone I couldn't really see any possible way they would keep Rashid, the man I was fast falling in love with. This man who had been my friend for two years, and my love for two months, surely he would be the one they would turn things around for, the one they would release early. Surely the ten years he had done *before* I'd known him was punishment enough. Surely now it was time to send him back out of prison and into my arms.

This is why I looked for him the way I did, always glancing around corners, checking faces on the subway, rushing anxiously home thinking that maybe. Maybe this day would be that day, the one when I would come home and find him there, in front of my apartment building, waiting, smiling.

It was a childish fantasy, I knew, not based in logic or reality. But that fantasy, sometimes it was all that could get me through, the idea that maybe today would be the day. If not, then perhaps the day after that, or the one after that. It was in this way that I would learn to measure Rashid's absence, to measure it and deflect its blows.

From very early on, Rashid's absence from the everyday of my life came out wild, swinging, some sort of renegade boxer. There were no rules, no referees. I had to structure a defense, one that I could sustain for this extended bout; when we fell in love, there was more than a decade left on his sentence.

Certainly though there were, in those initial weeks of ardent desire, these small spurts of nagging concerns when I wondered, What if he really has to do all this time, this whole other decade? Those moments, when they would come, it would feel like I had a choice, as though I was standing on the threshold between sanity and insanity. I couldn't figure out how to move, if to move, where I should go.

I couldn't imagine that the God I knew would have sent me the love I always wanted, the love I always needed, only to position it behind an unscalable wall. I prayed, I asked, *Was this my punishment for never being patient when I was a child? Was I to learn the lesson now, the one my mother tried but could not teach me, that patience is a virtue?*

When my fantasies would fail me as they sometimes did, the pain was free to snatch me up at gunpoint, make me walk a balance beam, not walk on it so much as run on it, jump on it. And maybe I would stay on and maybe I would fall off. I never knew, but either way, it made me exist within the fear that I had nearly no room to move. I used to think about falling off, how it could perhaps be a relief. No more fighting to keep balance. I thought these things, then, during week one, week two, week five, and week six of our relationship. I think these things, though less often now, in year eight of it.

But my fantasies, always they return to me, and still I walk home from the store, the gym, the poetry reading, the editor's meeting, thinking what if he's there, waiting on my stoop? What will I do? Will I faint, will I cry, will I scream, will I just grab him, pull him inside my apartment, and vow never to move from that space, that time?

They are like my own psychotropic prescription. They lift me, and although it is only for a moment, it's still enough to allow me to keep it and that I have, pushing on into the next letter, the next phone call, the next level of love, commitment.

I am not crazy. I am not crazy. It is right for me to love him. It is. It is.

I would chant these words when I awoke, chant them before I slept, chant them in the streets, chant them on the subways, over and over and over and over. I chanted until my chanting took on a physical form; it became something I could see, a picture, a painting. I saw our love in pastels bordered with brash dark oils. I could see this as if it hung on my wall, and for a time there was nothing else to be noticed, nothing else to be contemplated. I'm sure now that this is how they were able to advance on me, the years I've now spent going in and out of the prison. To advance, and then line up before me, poised, like some merciless firing squad.

on the road:
an update for the nineties

*t*he first time I visited Rashid not as a volunteer, but as a girlfriend, his girlfriend, it was the day after Christmas, the earliest part of the day, and I was sitting in a van, one of the many that a partner, a sister, a father or mother can take to get to one of the seventy prisons which are scattered across New York State.

Outside my window I watched morning pull reluctantly over the burnt edges of the South Bronx neighborhood, the place that served as the final stop the prison-bound van would make in the city before heading upstate. There was a coffee shop where we could go to the bathroom or buy breakfast. Most of the women piled out, and moments later, piled back in.

The van which transports up to fourteen people to the prison is always overwhelmed by the smell of bacon-and-egg sandwiches, coffee and hot chocolate, inexpensive perfume, hair pomade, nail polish, and skin laced with that last, desperately smoked cigarette. The air locks like a hangman's noose, a noose we have slipped our own necks into. The ride begins.

Two years into my relationship with Rashid, when he was transferred eight hours away from New York City, somewhere in north hell, to a facility that is walking distance from the Canadian border, and riding the van was not an option, I came to appreciate, even mourn its absence. The transfer, which was incorrectly ordered, was eventually overturned, but only after months and months of administrative and legal battles. And in the year before Rashid came back downstate, I learned how very nasty this life can get.

I learned from the very minute that I arrived at Columbus Circle in mid-Mahattan at 11 P.M. on one Friday night to meet the bus which would take me and several hundred other women to the faraway prison, the one up near Canada. And there, at Columbus Circle, waiting to head out, I was just half a mile from where I grew up. This is what I was struck by, standing in central Manhattan, under a midnight April rain: the proximity of the bus stop to my parents' house was far more predominant in my mind than that steady, cold showering, and the whimpering babies, and the impatient buzz of all those women, women like me, corralled, watching our faces fall down.

I fumbled in my bag for an umbrella and thought about how much my parents wanted to protect us, my sister and me, from anything and anyone and anyplace that would take away our choices, that would constrict our freedom. Private schools, summer camps, piano lessons, dance lessons, swimming, horseback riding, art classes, gymnastics, there was nothing my parents thought to refuse us if it would help us to become emotionally strong, independent women. What would they have said and what would they have felt if they'd seen me right then, about to board a bus where the first thing you're told is not the destination, but,

No cigarette or crack smoking on the bus, and no drinking no kind of liquor or beer.

When I was a teenager with no curfew, every weekend I roamed the streets of my neighborhood with my best friend Nicole, drinking beer and cheap wine, smoking cigarettes and spliffs, discussing nuclear destruction, sex, love, isolation, drugs, and music. Sometimes we would sit, the two of us, by the fountain at Lincoln Center. Other times we would wander over to Central Park, to the entrance at Fifty-ninth Street and Columbus Circle, past all of these women who were standing there amid boxes, bags, and babies, waiting to board buses that were headed to places we didn't know.

We knew nothing of prisons then, Nicole and I, as we passed the women nearly every Friday night. And as we passed, perhaps we whispered, but we never really wondered about them, the women, who they were, what they thought, what they were doing there. And we never feared, at least I never feared, that the sharp-edged world our parents tried to warn us about and protect us from could come slicing down into the heart of our dreams. Wherever Nicole is now, perhaps she is safe, perhaps she has avoided ever getting cut. I hope this is true, that she has never bled, in the way I have now bled, from the center of my life, from the very pulse of it.

But as a sad teenager who didn't see life past my twenty-first birthday, there was no way I could have ever predicted this moment when my life, the whole of it, was about to be pushed onto a bus and then squeezed into a seat which was not made to hold two grown people comfortably. Strangers we were, the woman and I stuffed in next to each other, swelled with stress, hoping to sleep for at least thirty minutes, an hour. We tried to sleep somehow without touching each other, without taking up space that didn't belong to us.

When Rashid was finally transferred back downstate, back within a two-hour drive from New York City, I called Freddie, my old van driver, and told him I'd returned. *Thank God,* I'd said. *Come get me, come pick me up,* I said, *on Thursday for a visit.*

He is a grumpy man, Freddie the van driver, but he is a good man, hardworking, like my father, exactly so. And being back on the van felt like coming home. I hated that it felt like that, but the familiar faces I saw in the seats, the door-to-door service, and Freddie holding open and closing the door for me, made me relax.

The first time I saw Freddie after the faraway upstate horror show, I wanted to hug him, but of course I didn't. In this world, it would be improper. It would be suggestive. With my man locked away, there are already suspicions that I, that women in my position, are lonely, even desperate. I simply said good morning to Freddie, as did he to me, although he mumbled his greeting. He grunted it almost.

Freddie, one of the women called out, *you got to open that window. And turn the music up too.*

I looked around at the women in the van, their young, old, and middle-aged faces were all locked up, just like mine. Their emotions were tucked into the corners and folds and wrinkles of their flesh. Their hairdos were protected by cotton-poly scarves, and their makeup was perfect. Their nails were long, curled, and colored. Their clothes, like my clothes, were, for the most part, their Sunday best. I absorbed those women, my sisters (myself), as though we were a masterpiece painting.

We were like an Easter Parade on crack.

the edge:
topography of a first date in a prison

When I went to see Rashid, we arrived for the six-hour visit at almost nine in the morning. Now, after these eight years of going up and back, the ride can feel endless, those four drawn-out hours from door to door. But my first time I was so excited and nervous, I thought we got there, to the prison, almost before I even found a seat in the van.

We pulled into the parking lot of the prison, the one I was so familiar with, the one that looked like a castle, the one I had been volunteering in for almost two years, the one which held Rashid. I followed the more experienced visitors up a long ramp, through two sets of unbelievably thick, heavy metal doors. It was not an entrance I had ever used before. But that was not the only thing which was different about this visit.

How I got treated by police had also changed; I was no longer a volunteer. I was a prisoner's lover now, his woman, his partner. Being a volunteer afforded me a tiny measure of courtesy, but being a lover, a girlfriend, afforded me mostly hostility and suspicion. Mothers, sisters, friends, fathers, cousins, and wives, all of us were treated with hostility and suspicion.

I entered a room with gray lockers and black plastic chairs, two bathrooms, a metal detector, and two police positioned behind a desk with no chairs. As instructed, I filled out a form, and when the police called my name, not my name, but Rashid's number, I walked over to the desk. I had put all of my things into a locker, except a change purse, a lipstick, a comb, and a pen. As a volunteer, I could always bring in my bag. As a visitor, the same bag became contraband. I handed over my change purse, form, and ID to an officer who did not look at me.

Remove your shoes, coat, and jewelry. Place them on the desk.

I did as I was told, and then began to walk through the metal detector.

Not yet! I was admonished. *Go back to the other side of the machine and wait until I'm ready.*

Pen and lipstick ain't allowed. I'll hold onto them until you come out or you can put them back in your locker. He said this, and then told me, *Now, go through the metal detector.*

I stepped through and it beeped.

Do it again and don't touch the sides.

I did as I was told, and went through once more without making a sound.

The officer motioned me through two electronically locked doors. The first one opened, and I stepped through. It closed, and then the second one opened, and I entered another large room with rows and rows of orange and black chairs, vending machines, and tables. I handed my entry form to an officer who was sitting at a desk in the front of the room. I took a seat at a table which was in the furthest corner of the room. I waited, nervous, feeling discomforted by the search process.

There would come a time a few years later when that search would seem like child's play, friendly almost. That time came after I married Rashid, and it would remind me of a story, a piece of history that had been trapped in my throat since I learned of it. It had been trapped there and it had been rotting.

It was the story of the Venus Hottentot. The first time I read about her, I did not know, I could not have known how she would follow me. But then the first time I read about the Venus Hottentot, the eighteenth-century Black South African woman who had been tricked into migrating to England, who had been stripped and forced into a British circus cage, who had been gawked at, talked about, trampled by a thousand hard, white eyes, I had never been inside a prison. What did I know then about cages, humiliation, forced exposure?

Getting processed into visiting rooms across New York State means police have the right to scan even my tampons and hold them up to the light. It is almost always men who do these searches. Almost every single time.

After we are married and granted conjugal visits, before I enter the trailer site where Rashid and I will spend our time, it will be my panties, diaphragm, and K-Y Jelly that male officers hold out in public often as a company of inmates is walking past five, maybe eight feet, from us. They have fingered my black silk panties, the ones I bought for only Rashid to see. They've shaken down my bra, my nightgown, even though it is sheer.

The first two or three times that happened to me, I felt immodest. I felt shame and embarrassment. Now I feel camaraderie with women who work the peep shows or who lap dance for a living. Except, of course, that I don't get paid. But you know I think I should. For every glance that gets held too long, for each time one of those police runs his fingers across my underwear, those motherfuckers owe me, in the very least, cash money.

≈

And then there was a morning when the wire in my bra set off the metal detector. The sergeant looked at my chest and then told me that,

Of course you don't have to go through this kind of search. But if you want to get this visit, you going to have open up your shirt and let the female officer scan you. In the bathroom of course. It's a normal security procedure and the directive's posted over there if you want to read it.

What choice did I have? I followed the female officer, a Puerto Rican woman who looked as though she could have been my mother, into the women's restroom. She did not want to search me any more than I wanted to be searched. She knew like I knew that it was completely unnecessary. A hand scanner could have been used over the top of my denim blouse. But in prison, those who have any modicum of power need neither logic nor decency to guide them through their decisions. Had I chosen to argue the point, even if I won, visiting hours would have been over.

Because she could not be hostile to the man who was her ranking officer, this female police was hostile to me. So much for sisterhood being global. It wasn't even local. In any case, as nasty as she got, barking orders as though *I* had offended her, her attitude had little impact on me.

Before I had even walked into that bathroom, I was gone, the soul of me was gone. It was disappeared out of my body. I was functioning but not present, split off and detached. It was a trick I had learned to do while having sex. It was an ancient trick; I could not remember a time when I did not know how to leave in this way.

My hands undid the first few buttons of my blouse, as my mind drew pictures on the walls, orange and green strokes dipped in screams. I saw myself dancing between the colors on the wall, uninhibited and unburdened. My body was see-through blue, a Caribbean ocean wave. I was rising in slow motion, all strength and untouchable, roaring, sky-bound, winged.

Lower, the officer said, *open your shirt up all the way. You're still beeping. And the jeans, take them down past your thighs.*

I unbuttoned, pulled down, turned forward and back. I out-stretched my arms, shook out my bra, all the while, all inside myself, I was chanting and singing, visualizing and meditating.

In the end I was left standing there with my shirt and bra open and my pants pulled down. And for all of that, contra-band was never found, nor was it ever really expected to be found. The reality is that if they truly feared I had some weapon stashed on me which was making the metal detector go off, why would they send me into a locked room with one of their unarmed officers, who was a woman twice my age and half my size?

All right, she growled, *get dressed and next time don't wear no underwire bra.*

I haven't worn anything but underwire bras since I was fif-teen, maybe fourteen years old. In the all the years that I have been going into the prisons and through the metal detectors, I have never worn anything but underwire bras.

But those machines can be adjusted to varying degrees of sensitivity, which always makes us, the visitors, wonder if the metal detector has as much to do with harassment and power than with security. *If this was about security,* I complained once to another woman who had also just gone through metal detector drama, *the machine would always register that I was wearing an underwire bra.*

Yup, she said. She nodded and poked out her lip, frustrated. *You right about that.*

I mean the thing would always be hypersensitive, unless of course the police felt it was okay to sneak knives or guns in one day, but not the next. You know what I'm saying, I continued, and she agreed.

Given this, it has, therefore, been no surprise to me that in the years since the incident, the years where all of my bras have had underwire in them, not once has the metal detector ever gone off again. Not once.

When I told Rashid what happened to me, I expected him to be outraged about it, but he wasn't. Disturbed, maybe. Sorry that I went through the search. But not livid, rushing to his word processor to pound out memorandums and complaints to officials in Albany.

At some point I realized why my ordeal must have seemed small in his eyes. After every visit he has with me or anyone else, my baby gets strip-searched, often by men who openly despise him. In a small cubicle, he is told to remove all of his clothes and shake them out. He is made to run his hands through his hair, to open his mouth wide, lift his tongue, lift his balls, turn around and squat, then stand again, display the bottom of his feet, and then turn back around and face the police. Once, while waiting to be processed, a female officer bragged to me and two other women about how she could strip-search a male inmate if she had to. *It's in the rules,* she said to us, grinning and confident.

When I learned about strip searches, what they entailed, I was shocked. My stomach knotted up. Whatever I had imagined did not live up to the description Rashid gave me, and I knew that despite the arguments that explained why such a process was necessary, I could never, ever do such a job. No matter what. I couldn't participate in that sort of humiliation. Not of anyone. Not at anytime. I wondered about the police who did it, day in and day out, especially the ones who could brag about it to wives and girlfriends. What did they go home and tell their children? *Daddy looks up men's assholes for a living.*

I realized that Rashid was not outraged by what happened to me because searches were something he was nearly desensitized to; humiliation is the daily fabric worn to fray in the life he leads and the life I was choosing to live along with him.

Both of us knew, we said this to each other, that we had a responsibility to fight some of the battles the prison system instigated, but if we fought every single one that was thrown our way, what time would be left to laugh or to dream, to hope or to just be at peace? And then who would be the real winners?

We take the experience and shove it deep down inside ourselves. We crush it like trash to be bagged, compacted, taken out, and eventually, incinerated.

Inspections, interrogations, suspicions, and searches, there's a kind of freedom in being forced to place yourself in the hands of people who hate you, have them hold you up to the light, scan you, scrutinize you. This is what I have come to believe, finally, that there is a purity in sharing when there's nothing left to hide, no spaces for modesty or retreat.

I know that Rashid understands me as no lover has. I know

I am unburdened with him, never worrying that he will find out the woman I really am, the woman I hid or tried to deny with every other man I have ever been involved with.

We play no games, tell no lies, have no camouflage, are as naked and displayed as the Venus Hottentot, Rashid and I. All we have, all we are, and all we hope to be is out on the table, dissected and documented. We can either wither apart and give in to the madness, or else struggle, keep honoring that, despite everything, we can still love and make the love feel good.

And we wear our love in the way long intersecting roots wear the earth. And we wrap it around ourselves the way I've seen children wrap blankets around themselves. Beautiful, thick cotton blankets from Mexico with familiar colors and insistent patterns. That is what our love looks like. And we pull ourselves tight and together, beneath blankets, beneath earth, and we are warmed through and through. In cold, stark visiting rooms, we whisper that this cannot last forever, and we are warmed.

During that first visit, however, I was not very wise about how to survive within the walls of a prison. The first time, I sat at a table as far away from the guard's desk as possible; I thought that this would give us privacy, but later I learned that I had positioned myself directly in front of a two-way mirror. But that morning, sitting there dressed all in white, I did not consider such invasions, only the artifice and oddities of that large room with its plastic plants and its plastic chairs, the children scurrying everywhere, the women breathing back their tears, and all those men, those mostly Black men, those mostly strong, handsome men moving uncomfortably through the space in ugly, green, state-issued pants.

Suddenly there was a loud, jarring buzz, and then a door near to me opened and Rashid walked through. I recognized him immediately, although just the night before, when I had tried for several minutes, I found I could not call his face to me. I could not see it there, behind my eyes.

It was his voice, his handwriting, that I had come to know intimately. How to assign them, now, to that mouth, to that right hand? He greeted me, Rashid did, with a smile as big as the time he has served in these stone walls. I smiled back, but I did not stand, and I did not move. I did not know what I should do. In the two years that we had been friends, we had never hugged tightly, nor kissed, nor held each other's hands. In the two years that we had known each other, I could not remember a time when we had ever once touched for any more than a few brief seconds. Yet here we were, somehow together, in this bizarre place, having declared our love, but having never embraced.

I should kiss him, full, my mouth in his mouth.

That was what I thought as he approached me.

I should hold him, pull him to me so that he can feel all the passion in my twenty-five-year-old body.

I should run my hands through his hair, ease my fingers down his back.

I should whisper sexy things into his ear.

I thought those things, but I did not act on them. I did not move and I did not speak, until Rashid said,

Hey, girl, can I get a hug?

And I rose, I took him in my arms, not in the way that I

wanted to, but in the way that I felt was appropriate. I embraced him only lightly. I did not push my body hard into his. He kissed me on my cheek.

We were restrained, both of us, but for a long time after the hug was over, we continued standing. We stood and we held hands, and if either one of us had had the courage to have spoken right then in those slow minutes, we would have said, *I love you.* I am sure of this.

We would have said it with all the conviction we had said it in letters and even on the phone. But this was different, unlike the calls and letters, we were at once without barrier or boundary. My eyes were firm upon his eyes and there was no turning back. That visit seemed to be the difference between talking about how much you wanted to skydive, talking about it for months and months, and then finally the day coming, and you are there, being told to get over by the open door of the plane. Courage can take a walk in that moment, it can curl up in a corner, curl up into a place where you can no longer see it.

This was how we were: perched at the edge of a airplane, thousands of miles above an expansive and unknowable landscape, wondering, when the time came, would our parachutes work, would all those lessons, the ones we'd learned that had brought us to this day, be in any way useful, if we took a deep breath, and if we said a prayer, and if we closed our eyes and if we just did it, if we went ahead, if we jumped?

conversations, 1: the fall

*i*f you're going to survive in prison, when you come in you got to be cool for a minute. Just watch until you can read the script, see what's up.

On our first visit I was full of questions about Rashid, about prison, about survival. We were sitting at the table. We were sitting very close. Our legs touched and a chill coasted down my back and as I was riding this chill, Rashid said he wanted me to know all about his case. In front of us were his transcripts.

You need to know if you're going to be with me.

I did not know then about prison protocol, how people rarely discuss their crimes even with their wives. Sometimes I talk to women now, women who ride the vans with me. They tell me how little they know about their husband's case, how they ask and ask, and how he won't divulge details beyond the nature of the crime.

What Rashid was doing on our first visit was setting up a foundation of honesty and trust. I see this now, but then I was not ready, and I did not understand. I was not prepared for Rashid, the man I was beginning to love, the man I was beginning to enjoy loving, to evaporate, and in his place, have a killer appear.

Can we talk about other things first?

I nearly pleaded this, and Rashid agreed, and instead began explaining prison life to me.

Things here will get pretty clear to you—eventually—but if you

*rush, you'll make mistakes and offend somebody, and then it's a big
fight and who needs that, you know what I mean?*

*When I first got locked down, I moved real easy. One of the things
I noticed right away was how brothers acted in the mess hall. Okay,
for example, you might be sitting at a table with somebody you don't
know, so the whole time, you're not talking, it's total silence, but still
you would never just get up or turn your back to him. When you get
ready to do that, you knock on the table twice. Like this.*

Rashid knocked, two fast, hard raps, on our visiting room
table.

Really? I said.

Yeah. You know where that comes from? he asked. But before I
could respond, he continued,

*Back in the day, police couldn't speak to inmates so they used to
knock on walls with their batons to signal when to stop and when to
go. One knock meant stop, two meant go. So prisoners just got that
into their way of communicating. Not speaking, but banging. All of
us do it.*

Right then, we were interrupted by a couple who was passing by our table. Rashid introduced them and told me afterwards that the young man was locked in a cell near his. He told
me that they were becoming friends.

What'd he do? I asked.

I don't know, baby.

But he's your friend.

*Yeah, but we don't speak about that. Dudes don't speak about
their crimes too tough in here. I mean it's just not done. The only
reason for me to know would be like, say, if I was helping him with
his case.*

The only reason? I challenged. *What if he was a rapist or a child
molester?*

Come on now, baby. People with that kind of case, you know about, and obviously I wouldn't mess with him.

What if he was a wife beater? What if he killed his wife? Is killing a woman better than raping her?

And that question hung between us by a thin rope until finally it fell, a loud, violent, crashing fall. Pieces sprayed everywhere. I picked up some of the pieces and Rashid picked up some of them, but still there was this mess. Frustrated, we walked away from it. We said we would come back. We said we would clean it up later.

conversations, 2:
did you drive away fast,
did you drive away slow?

*d*id terrible dreams come split the night and render it useless, unsalvageable? Did you wake up with a start, the way they do in movies? Did your sweat drip down the air? Did your breath go tight? Did you slope into the morning, like a tired, unwilling guest?

Did you make love to your woman? Did you kiss her more intensely? Did you stare at her nipples before you put them in your mouth? Did she become uncomfortable with you staring? Did she tell you *Please just do it, Poppi, I can't wait any longer?* Did you tell her she would have to? Did you say if you went slow, you always would remember?

And did you? Remember?

Did you dance, man? Did you put Luther on the stereo? Did you pull your woman out of bed, and wrap your arms around her waist, and was it your naked arms, and was it her naked waist? Did you sing along with Luther when he said *A chair may be a chair, but a house is not a home if no one's living there?*

Did you run your hands along your books and records, along the fabric of your couch, along the clothes hanging in your closet? Did you jingle your keys? Did you lock and unlock your door? Did you throw your window open, stick your head outside unrestricted?

Did you see your boys on the corner? Did you go and give them each a pound? Did you all smoke cigarettes together? Did you all smoke a spliff? Did you ride around the block and say you thought the South Bronx was really beautiful? Did your boys say *'Cuzz you crazy, better leave that weed alone?* Did you laugh when they said this? Was your laughter a lie?

Did you drive out to Jersey so that you could see your son? Did you kiss him, did he gurgle, did you whisper that you love him? Did you leave his mama money? Did you tell her go buy herself something nice? Did she notice you seemed different? Did you say, yes? Yes.

Did you drive away fast, did you drive away slow? Did you look into your rearview mirror and see no reflection looking back? Did you feel terrified in that moment, all gangster bravado crumbled? Did you take a look again, in the mirror that did not reflect you, and did you scream, that second time, did you scream, did you know?

What did you do on the day they came and got you, the day you were arrested? Was there some sort of foreboding? Did you feel that it was coming?

I ask these questions of Rashid when we first become a couple, and for a long time he considered them.

You never see it coming, asha. This is what he says. *There wouldn't be so many people dead, and there wouldn't be so many people here, if we could ever see it coming.*

conversations, 3:
the charge was murder

*t*he charge was murder in the
second degree. The man who was killed had been somebody's
husband. He had been somebody's father. Rashid was nineteen years old, and acting in concert with his big brother and
an older man named Lou. The transcripts told me this.

*The man had been Lou's partner. Lou said he was robbing him,
and that upset me because Lou was sort of like my father.* Rashid
told me this.

*But I was a little afraid of him, Lou, I mean. The thing was once
he told me what was planned, I guess I felt if I backed out Lou might
get me too.*

Rashid paused, and then,

Not that that's an excuse. It's just the way it was.

And that was what I wanted to know most of all, how it
was, everything, the day itself, what was it like? I demand to
know from Rashid, was it hot like the hot they say that can
drive a man crazy? Was it cold, a mean, icy, stinging, wet cold?
Was the moon full? When we did discuss the case in its entirety,
I found I needed something to explain it beyond what had
been recorded by the courts. *Give me some reason, some huge,
terrible, beyond-your-control reason.* I urged Rashid, I begged
him, I implored, *Tell me, tell me,* but he offered me nothing. He
said only that,

*I can barely remember the day. Not in details like you're asking,
asha. All these years, I've tried not to think of it. Thinking of it is*

worse than doing the bid, if you can believe that. It's worse. That's why I had to get rid of that person, that man I used to be. As much as possible, I had to block out all the bad stuff from those days. If I didn't it would have driven me insane. I'm telling you, girl, I would have been a lunatic.

I understood that and I told Rashid so. I told him and then let it go for the moment. We began to discuss other things, small things, lovers' things. We held each other. We moved on. At 3:30 the guard announced that visiting hours were over. We embraced before I left, and as I turned to walk toward the door, Rashid asked me to wait a second.

After, I threw up and was in bed for days. I remember that. I remember that.

❧

It never goes away, not forever, the murder. No matter what we do, no coercion or coaxing, no bribe, no begging, no physical force, no slap or scream, no denial, no good deed, no belief in God, or life or love, can make it go away. At best, it retreats for a time, at best.

Once, in the middle of a discussion about children, how we love them, both of us do, I just inserted the question. I asked Rashid, how did he manage to confront it?

You can't possibly just block it out all the time, can you? I posed this as a question, but it was an accusation, really. *How do you deal with it?*

Without having the choice to do anything else.

Rashid's voice was flat, but not sarcastic. He was looking the other way from me.

And I pray. I pray for forgiveness.

From who? From her? I asked, *From his wife?*

From God, he responded, and then,

I don't know how to ask her. But I've tried to anyway. In my prayers I've asked. I've prayed for her forgiveness. And his too. The child's, I mean. The man's son. His son, and also my own son. He pulled his lips together tight, Rashid did, and he nodded his head slowly, and then he stopped speaking.

That was when I changed the subject. Again. Like always. Eventually, I always just change it.

conversations, 4:
visions, visitations

*t*he way I've learned to look at the crime is in small pieces, never as a whole. As a whole it would be too big. Taken all at once, it could knock me over, it could knock the breath out of me. I knew this immediately, which is why I crept up on it the way I did, one section at a time, from the back to the front, from the Rashid of today to the Rashid of yesterday.

There are young people who come into the prisons as part of a program designed to get them off the path of juvenile delinquency and steer them away from crime forever. Rashid heads this program. He has for years now. Sometimes when he talks about it, he tells me that he understands how those young people hurt, not just how, but also where.

That's why they love you, I tell him. *Why so many of them say you saved their life.*

I say this to Rashid, thinking of the letters that have been written to the prison both about him and the youth program. Rashid nods his head, and then almost smiles and then looks down. And when he does this, these three subtle movements, I know he is embarrassed. He is less interested in accepting my compliments, or the compliments of the young people, than he is in simply being polite enough to acknowlege that I have spoken. My partner is, he has become, a very humble man.

And I close my eyes around that image, the one of my life-saving partner, my generous partner, my modest partner, my loving partner. I paste it up, make it a permanent part of my sight. And I go to it, the current image of Rashid, that picture, when I can no longer avoid the murder or the face of a killer.

≈

There were these times when it was very, very still and very, very late that she would come to me, the widow, the woman left behind. Quiet, that's how she always was, never imposing, and never mean. She would come to me in my room, the one which was filled with pictures of Rashid and me holding each other, Rashid and me in love. She would sit there on my bed, and she would look at me, but it wasn't hostile, her look. It was a curious sort of look, one that asked questions, one that wondered, perhaps, who I was, who Rashid was, for me to love him the way I did.

I would always meet her eyes at every visitation. It was the least she deserved, this is what I felt, the very least, indeed. When she came, I would look at her levelly and continuously, until whenever she'd choose to leave. It was not an easy thing to do, never. But every time I managed to do it, to hold her gaze steady, woman to woman across a history cut short and cut jagged, I would feel rooted more deeply in the love I'd been given.

If I could still love Rashid in that moment when I was looking in her face, could we possibly be wrong then, could we possibly be a lie? I would ask her these questions, I would whisper them to her each time she'd come, but she would never answer me, and she would never stay.

the place we go to,
the way we get there

from the very beginning of our relationship, we have danced, Rashid and I, there in the visiting room, between the plastic tables and the plastic chairs, and beside the daylight that fails, that falters behind those old venetian blinds shut tight and weighed down by years of dust, years and years of it. We dance slow, and we dance steady, and I sing in his ear, and if anyone, other visitors or prisoners or even the police, if any of them have looked upon us as though we are strange, we have never noticed it.

In that room, all of us, with all of our differences and all that separates us, we still know this one thing. We know that to survive in prison we have to transform not only ourselves, but our spaces, our imaginations, that table, this chair, everything must change, everything.

This is what I think about, not always, but sometimes, when we are dancing, and when the visiting room is becoming our private room, and the bars have fallen away, and the doors and the locks have crumbled, and nothing and no one exists except our two bodies, our brown eyes, our locked hands, our barely moving feet, and the music we make together. That's all, nothing else is there, not one other thing.

What is the moment your life changes course forever? One afternoon I was holding onto Rashid as we danced, and that question came to me. I wondered how you would know that moment to identify it, to grab it up out of the air? I thought it probably wouldn't be the obvious one, the moment that announces its arrival, the one that crashes and splatters, the one we would note in our journals, and tell our friends about, and tell strangers even. If it were indeed that moment, I thought, then we could control it as it started to race toward us. We could make the decision to either get out of the way or else embrace it.

Later I argued that point to a friend. I said to her how you're never conscious of the moment of irrevocable change, but she told me I was wrong. She said it was indeed the big moment, the one of the impact. I asked her to imagine that she was crossing a street and then suddenly a drunk driver sped by and hit her as she stepped off the curb. What was the moment of change, I asked her? Was it the moment when the car hit, or the moment when the driver got behind the wheel, or when he started drinking that night, or when she, my friend, went outside, out onto the curb?

Dancing with Rashid has made me believe that my life didn't change when I told people it changed. My life changed long before the first phone call, or letter, or visit, and I now wonder if perhaps it was when I saw that my ex-husband would never make himself a great emotional presence in my life, and I realized I would need that. I would need it more than I needed a physical presence even, more than sleeping next to a man every night, more than sitting across a dinner table from him every evening.

Perhaps that moment of realization was when my life changed, but perhaps not. Perhaps my moment of change happens every time Rashid takes me in his arms and holds me tightly in the room we have made our own room, and begins to move himself and move me to the quiet rhythm of the music that we are playing in our own heads, and somehow, somehow, we begin to exist only in the freedom of the imagination we are sharing, as though we are one mind and one body, one vision and one thought riding the back of the sun to a place in ourselves that no one else will ever be able to see or separate, or touch or take away, or isolate or imprison.

when i was a child

*R*ashid and I always came back to this discussion on transformation, the possibility of it. It was an idea that spiraled inward; we began with the need for reform in the prison and in the world outside, but the more we talked, the more we found the need to focus on the world inside. We became mirrors for each other.

Of course Rashid needing and wanting to transform was obvious. His history demanded this of him. But I was not without my own issues and they also required examination, their own process of transformation. This was not immediately apparent, however, and at first I suppose I did just sort of bask in the admiration Rashid had for me.

After doing all those programs in the prisons, after hearing all my poems and politics, Rashid had constructed me as this strong, sharp, independent woman, a woman with a tongue made of fire who could argue back the dark. I was, in his eyes, a woman with a spirit made of steel, an unbreakable woman.

And certainly it did, this image, have its bits of truth, as much as any illusion holds some truth in the eye of the believer, which Rashid was, and perhaps I was as well. I believed the masquerade that I had, myself, created. And not only did I believe it, I counted on it, on her, the pretend asha. I had envisioned her not as my understudy but as my replacement; just like in the movies, she would step out of the shadow of the chorus and take over for me. (I had collapsed somewhere offstage.)

Almost from the minute she emerged, the audience went

wild for the replacement asha. She had so much more confidence than I, so much more stamina. She could take the midair leaps that my legs always refused. She was the more dramatic performer, the funny one, the one with so much more charm, the one people remembered with a smile.

I got used to her being me, Rashid and I both did, and this was why it was completely devastating when she left the show, and I was forced to return to myself without any warning, and without any direction, and without even any rehearsal.

This is how it happened:

Rashid and I decided that we would tell each other everything, that there would never be any secrets between us. We didn't know then what that would mean, how it would strip us, leave us before each other without weapons, shields, masks.

This is what we knew:

Telling everything was the only way to understand how we could ever have arrived at this place. We believed it was the only way we would figure out how we would go from it one day, and, as George Jackson said, *leave nothing behind.*

When we talked, we discovered we could travel out of the prison, sometimes out of America. The fullness of our communication became, and still is, the road out of the prison, the road back home.

Will you take me to Guyana?

I asked Rashid this on one Tuesday visit when it was raining outside and we were leaning into each other and we were whispering. Rashid said he would take me to Guyana. He said,

Of course. As soon as I'm home, we're going to go.

No, I corrected. *I mean now. Can you take me there now?*

And he did, he took me there. He drew me the most incredible, the most vibrant and detailed picture of growing up in Guyana. And I could feel it, and I could taste it, and I could see it, and I could smell it, the splash and salt of that heated green sea. And I could see him there, Rashid.

I could see the way it once was: him, a small boy playing, running, making mischief, and all the mothers scolding him, and all the old men playing dominoes on corners, the boys scampering up the coconut trees, the girls in their Catholic school uniforms, and everywhere green, and mountains, and the tiny family shops, and wide, wide marketplace, and even the poverty, but the being together, at least that, the unity and symmetry of that world.

The way the prison had it, Rashid started and stopped in one moment, in one place, as a criminal, a convict, but I knew there was more. I knew his picture stretched back thirty years. And I knew his picture was a complex construction of color and lighting. Every time I looked at it I could find something different, and this is why I knew I needed to leave it hanging there on my wall where I could go back and study it, again and again.

I wish I never came to this country.

Rashid never said this to me, to say it would have been a sort of renunciation of our love, but I knew he must have thought it, even if it would have meant there would have been no us. And we were, so quickly, after the first few exchanges, with our openness, and our need, already, an us.

Yes, he and I, a couple, although there were no double dates, no Saturday nights at the movies. The only proof we had, the only tangible proof, was our communication, and we clung to it; in our relationship, it became exalted. When we were on the phone, I would close my eyes, and I would press my cheek closer into the receiver. It was an instinctual reaction; I wanted to be nearer to him, and in a way, when I made this almost imperceptible gesture, I was. On the inside, I was.

During those early phone calls, I would curl up in my bed and light my candles and burn my incense and play Coltrane's "Greensleeves," and refuse to allow the prison to be the sole arbitor of the atmosphere in which we had to live, in which we were going to build this love. Even now, not always, but often enough, there are quiet horns blowing from my CD player and incense and candles burning, a tenuous peace.

Talking with Rashid on the phone or in person made me think about how all my life I had walked into love like I was walking into a war zone, into a land that had been mined. I tried to move in camouflage, with guns strapped to my waist and a first-aid kit in a bag on my back. I felt every step made me more vulnerable, and eventually I would freeze. Eventually, I would stop going forward. I could not remember ever being another way.

Before Rashid, I could never rest with love, I could never relax with it, never fall back into its arms. I didn't trust the thing. With Rashid everything was so different. I was able, from our very first conversation, to be open with him, completely, to be all of who I was, the best and worst of who I was, and it felt strange, but it did not feel frightening. I was not scared, not even when we first started. I loved him from the first day. I loved him without any protective gear.

Rashid and I had been friends before we had been lovers. We loved each other intimately before we touched each other intimately, and I am sure this is what broke my defenses down without my even flinching; it never occurred to me or to him that there was any other way for us to be with each other except open, vulnerable.

I'm sure, too, what made a difference was that I felt that Rashid's own history would keep him from judging mine. I would conclude this finally when I began to wonder, out loud, in the presence of my lover, how I had become the woman I was. Why had I been so afraid for so long, so untrusting, so uncomfortable in my relationships? A book I was reading at the time told me that in order to explore every part of myself, in order to seek answers and resolution, I would have to be in a place where I could feel nurtured, at home. I knew that place was with Rashid, not just with him, but inside him, all the way, alongside his veins and heart and lungs. I was there, he was too, we both were.

Still, no matter how open, no matter how willing our hearts were, I have to confess that it was not only us. The prison itself played a significant role in solidifying how we were with each other, how close we would become. The prison, with all of its efforts to keep us unsteady, uncomfortable, and unable to love, became my adversary. Its stance against love automatically made me take a stance for love; I became a warrior. When I went to war, then, initially I thought I was battling against the bars and steel, the chains and cells, the brutal separation. I was a fierce soldier.

After enough time had passed that I was allowed some perspective, I came to see the battles quite differently, however. When all of my tactics and strategies had played out, when I had cursed and kicked and called the police all kinds of names, in the end the only one left in ruins was me. When the shock of seeing myself destroyed wore off, I realized it was not so terrible.

The me who had been killed was the me who had gone through life with shifty eyes, the ones that always greeted love sideways, looking at it askance, always as a potential enemy. I tell Rashid this, about how I had once looked at love, and he said he understood. He said that it was how he felt once, before me, before us. This was how we came to see ourselves as rebels.

We vowed a lifetime of battles against anything and anyone who tried to block our love from coming. We vowed a lifetime of battles against anyone or anything who could grab hold of our arms and pull us onto dangerous roads. And as we made our vows in the presence of ourselves and our ancestors and our God and the guards, we felt our apprehensions and our inhibitions come loose, and there they were and there we were, spilled like the pieces of two complex puzzles.

We stared at and played with those jumbled pieces of ourselves, the pieces which were piled on top of each other, the pieces that would get stuck sometimes on the wrong side of the puzzle. It would be a long time before everything fit together properly, years before things made sense. But that initial process of discovery, it was the most exciting thing, as though we were on the verge of uncovering some kind of miracle cure.

I wanted to know everything about Rashid, I told him this over and over. I wanted to know every twist, every turn. Nothing should be left out, I said to him, and he complied. Rashid told me stories about a double-faced childhood; a beautiful country that loved and nurtured him, but a country where men too often beat everything in their path, including women and children.

In Guyana that's just the way it was.

Oh, God.

And my mother left when I was a baby.

Why didn't she take you?

I don't know.

Come on. Don't tell me she just left you alone?

No. She left me in a suitcase. By my grandmother. That's what they say.

And then?

And then eventually we were all together again. Me and my brother with my father and his new family.

The stories Rashid told were like happiness in a crate turned upside-down and shaken out of position. What would begin as multicolored, as rainbow tales about a little boy and the ocean and the countryside and secret hiding places, would end up monochromatic, painfully dull, sometimes the swelled purple of bruises, sometimes the mean scarlet of skin ripped off of bare backs, bottoms, and legs.

I would push and Rashid would talk, and the colors in the stories slipped, each one of them fell on their backs and slid together. Purple into scarlet into finally only black. But at least it was a safe black, Rashid told me. It was a shadow black, a black like the black of the second before you pass out, and then nothing. No colors, no shadows, no thing at all.

That's why I used to run away a lot. I wasn't trying to be bad, but things were hard, asha. I can't even tell you.

Don't tell me, I wanted to but never did say. I never took my hand from in front of my mouth. I held it there, held every whimper and every scream there, there, locked behind my palm and my teeth. I held it, although now I think I should have let it free. But then I believed that if Rashid wasn't yelling, how could I? If he could disappear his emotions, then so could I, and that was what we did together. We walked through the stories of his youth as though they were normal, the everyday bread of life. Except once. Once I said finally,

I hate your family.

No, Rashid argued. *No, asha. Don't say that. Don't feel that way. It was a different time and place. It's just the way things were. It wasn't abuse. If it was, it wasn't on purpose. But I remember that once I did drink turpentine.*

Turpentine?

Yeah. Better to be dead. Know what I mean?

You tried to kill yourself?

I don't know about all that. I just didn't want to get a beating.

There's a difference between wanting to die and not wanting to live. I believe this and I said it to Rashid. I said it to him because suddenly as he talked about the turpentine, I remembered something from my own childhood. I remembered a time when I wanted to die, and then I remembered other times when I simply didn't want to live. Wanting to die is an active stance, an offensive play. It involves planning, consideration. Not wanting to live is a passive play. And a passive play as opposed to a defensive play. Even a defensive play is more bold. Not wanting to live is simply a retreat.

The story of Rashid being nine and drinking turpentine, the way it hit me, triggered first a sympathetic ache, and then an empathetic ache, and then a watershed of memory. And memory in a way I wasn't used to having memory. Memory with minute details, faces, sounds.

Whenever we would talk and Rashid would describe his childhood, I would get an uncomfortable sensation throughout my body. My head would hurt. All of his memories going far, far back were virtual snapshots of people and places he hadn't seen in fifteen years.

How do you remember all that? I'd ask, trying not to sound defensive. For some reason, I didn't know why—knowing would come later—my own memories of childhood were disconnected and sketchy at best, but most often they were stolen.

My memories were mostly stories I had snatched out of my mother's mouth, my sister's. When my family would all be together at Christmas, I would have them repeat the same old tales again and again. Afterwards, alone, I would try to record them forever in some sacred, safe place in my brain, but it never worked. There were leaks, there were holes, there must have been! I couldn't contain the stories of my childhood for any meaningful amount of time, no matter how hard I would try.

When Rashid and I were in a conversation, and my turn would come to tell some story, some detail of my own life, I would speak in big, broad terms. I hoped Rashid would not notice, no one else ever seemed to notice before, not even me. Even I hadn't noticed the the difficulty I had in retaining experiences, especially experiences with men, until this relationship. Before Rashid, no one, not me, not my first husband or my best friend, not my sister, not anyone I knew, ever dwelled much on the past. We all lived in the current moment, or the moment coming just then, from right around the corner.

With Rashid, things were different. Time had, in a sense, frozen in 1983, the year he was arrested. The streets and subways, his home, his cars, his hangout partners, his women and escapades, everything stopped at that moment in January when he was hauled off to jail. To stay alive, to be an entity existing beyond the walls of the prison, he had to go back. Going back, telling me who he was before the strip searches, the cells, and the number instead of the name, allowed Rashid to hold onto his humanity. It was proof that once he had been, and in time, he would be again, a man, whole, in control of his environment and himself.

But when it was my turn to talk, I was scared Rashid would think I was somehow holding back on him in spite of our promise to tell everything, to travel with each other back down the years. If Rashid's life was a feature film, mine was a trailer. Mine had no dialogue, no clear storyline. I tried to fill in the gaps with long, thorough descriptions of my Manhattan neighborhood, my academic parents, the private schools, the ballet lessons and art classes, but I knew the picture was hazy.

I knew the picture was, in fact, less like a film and more like an unfinished collage, maybe not unfinished, but one in which pieces had been torn out, photographs had come unglued and blown away. This is why the turpentine story became so significant. It triggered in me not just one picture, but a whole photo album of pictures, color and black-and-white, slides, and blown-up prints, in focus, detailed. When Rashid told me that he drank the poison, I told him that,

I tried once. I said this fast, nervous.

Tried what? He thought that I meant that I drank turpentine too. I could tell by the tone his voice had taken.

I tried to die.

You did? Rashid said, his voice coated with surprise and disbelief. *What'd you do, asha?*

I took pills. But before that, I can't remember when, only that it happened, I cut my wrists. It wasn't too deep though. I got scared when I saw the first little bit of blood. And plus it hurt. I was trying to end hurting.

As we talked I remembered things I hadn't thought of in years. I saw them, and my eyes became a movie screen, and there it was, scene one, my college dorm room, and me at sixteen, swallowing twenty-five, maybe thirty pills. And there it was, scene two, the pills going down and I was not feeling sick, just lonely, isolated. I was aching for my faraway best friend and aching about my irreverent lover. I was just aching. And then there is a fast cut to my smug college roommate. This was scene three. My college roommate who had read my journal while I was in the hospital and told other people what it contained. She told them how crazy she thought I was. Someone eventually told me what my roommate had done, and for several years after that, I would record nothing of my life anywhere, not on paper, not inside myself, nowhere.

But on the night of the pills, when I still thought our friendship and trust was intact, my roommate came back into our room. I didn't know she was going to come back in the room. She was supposed to have been at a party, but had forgotten something. I surmised this later, but I did not know for sure. I never did know for sure why she came back in that night, at that time. Immediately after the pills and the hospital stay, I left school, and my roommate and I did not keep in touch. I assume I had been told of her betrayal and just did like the Peter Tosh song says to do: *Walk and don't look back.* Anyway, I told Rashid, I could not remember the exact sequence of things then, but I remembered that roommate, that girl, how she came back in the dorm, how she saw me, and how she screamed. She stood over me, and she just screamed.

I was lying in the floor almost passed out. Someone, not my roommate, called an ambulance. While we were waiting for it to arrive, other students, and the dorm monitor, came into my room and slapped me. They slapped me and they pulled me up and they made me walk in order to keep me awake, conscious. I went up and down the hallway, a woman on each side of me, holding me up. And I did, I stayed conscious, conscious enough to feel embarrassed because I had made myself a spectacle. I had been trying to go away, to extirpate myself, to somehow never be seen again, and instead I found that I had only succeeded in making myself more visible.

And being more visible was something I had not counted on. I never imagined that a possible conclusion to swallowing the pills was being rescued. And I certainly never imagined the particular kind of rescue that drags you up and down a public hallway while you are wearing only a nightgown. When I told Rashid the story, I told him that if I thought about it hard enough, which I rarely did, I could still feel that industrial hallway rug scraping beneath my bare feet. I could still feel the bruises pushing out onto my skin in the same place where the women held the upper part of my arms tight, tight, pulling, pulling. I told Rashid,

They didn't have to pump my stomach at the hospital, you know. They only had to make me vomit; they make you vomit if it's soon enough after you've taken the pills.

I told him about the doctor, a Jamaican woman, who tended to me. She was the first of two Black doctors who had ever treated me. This was probably why I have remembered her so well, why I can still see her face, not all the way, but her general features.

She was the one, I said, *she told me that, about the vomiting and pills.*

She'd told me that as she sat on my bed, in a room with a camera in it that stayed trained on me for twenty-four hours like a wagging finger or else a gun.

Why'd you do it, asha? Rashid asked me this. It would be the first of many times he asked me that question.

I don't know, I said. *I was sad,* I said.

Nothing felt right, I added. *It was as though the entire world was misplaced. It was as though I was misplaced. I had been skipped and so I graduated from high school at fifteen. I was really too young to head off to college. But you couldn't have convinced me of that then. So when I got there—the school was in D.C.—I knew right away I didn't fit in that setting. I didn't even last a whole semester. From the moment I arrived, I felt like I was living in the wrong time in the wrong place, making mostly the wrong friends, and always falling for the wrong man.*

Nothing felt right, I said again, because I began to feel sure. *I was always thinking that, how nothing felt right,* I remembered aloud. I remembered wanting to die because I was thinking that.

After that, I told Rashid, I tried again. I took some pills again, *but it was six years later and it wasn't like before. I never tried as hard as I had tried that first time.*

The second time, I began, and as I did, I also began to gain an understanding I did not previously have, *the second time I didn't want to die so much as I didn't want to live.*

It came back to me, how the life I was living was so pointedly lonely; lonely because my first husband and I had come apart. We were there, living together, but still apart. We were in a house with no conversations over the dinner table, no evening walks, no sharing of problems, no touching, no tenderness. And then, at twenty-two years old, I didn't really know another way to leave except by dying. But it didn't mean that that's what I wanted, to die, only that I didn't want to live in emptiness.

That's the difference between wanting to die and not wanting to live. Does this make sense? I asked Rashid.

I think so. He said this slowly after a long pause, and then continued, *Yes, it does,* he said. *Yes.*

One morning not long after Rashid and I had fallen in love, I woke up and at first everything seemed as it had been before I'd closed my eyes and faded into sleep. But the appearance was a mirage and I realized this, the trick, when I left my Brooklyn apartment, and began the five-minute walk down Fulton Street, down toward the train station.

As usual, there were crack vials littering the ground, like bread crumbs that lead you into, not out of, the threatening forest. I was counting the vials, counting them and losing count of them when all at once, for reasons I did not understand then and do not understand now, I heard a voice. It didn't fit the moment, that voice. It was incongruous, out of place, ancient and abstract. It was also familiar and it played like a note repeating on a scratched record. Again and again I heard a man saying to me, *I taught you how to neck. I taught you how to neck.*

I listened and I listened for more and more words, but nothing else came. But the voice in my head, the voice of the man, said nothing else, and I said nothing at all. I was not part of a dialogue. I was just there, silent, staring at him. I remembered that suddenly. And I remembered I was seven or eight, a small girl visiting my mother's office in the big building on the college campus where the man taught, where the man took me off into a classroom and showed me math tricks, and then asked me to sit in his lap, which I did. I did it because I liked him, everybody liked him. And this was probably why I did not scream or question or move when his hand began to travel up my leg, up my thigh, and then whatever memory should have come right after that, did not. Everything stops with the moving hand. Everything except when the man and I were walking across the campus, and he said to me that now I knew *how to neck.*

On the day these memories came to me I called my mother. I called her when I got to work and told her what I remembered. I described the man and she told me his name. She told me that she could not believe that he would have done such a thing, and when she told me this, that she could not believe it, I said simply, *Me, either.* But what I thought about was the pervasive sadness that haunted me for so long. I thought about the drugs and the drinking. And I thought that my life stood as irrefutable testimony that somewhere, something had turned down a wrong and dangerous path, and finally I was going to have to face it. Finally I was going to have to understand why.

Months and months after that day on Fulton Street in Brooklyn I read a book about sexual abuse and the book taught me that repressed memories often come back at a time when you are best able to confront them. The book said that memories often surface when you are emotionally strong enough to confront them, or when you have support systems around you, or when you feel safe, and maybe that's true.

Maybe Rashid being a presence in my life then, emotionally consistent, nonabusive, and loving as he was, allowed me to be able to face that which had contorted me for so many years. But I can only speculate on this, because when the memories came, they were so rude and so nasty that there was no time or space or energy to wonder why. They had just come, that's all. And they were uncontained, and uncontainable, those memories. They burst in at any time they wanted to, wherever I was. They would step right up and stand in front of me. They would block my vision and they would distort it. They made friends seem like enemies. I fought with everyone who was in my proximity, especially Rashid.

When they came, those memories, they were fast as the water converging into a truculent, unpredictable sea. Those memories, they were like waves that were strong enough to erode a beach and erase a landscape. Erase it forever.

≈

There was never any question that something had happened to me, but what was it that had happened, and who was it that I should blame? This was the confusion that took over my life, and cornered my sun, and kept me moving in shadows, bumping into my past and breaking pieces of myself.

Of course I understood that the man from the college was wrong, because I was, after all, so very young then. But surely he, that man, could not have been enough to disintegrate my childhood and leave it as ashes and soot. Not one man alone.

I cannot remember, I cannot remember.

I would cry this to Rashid, that nothing was clear. I would tell him I could not find answers, only more questions. *I am frustrated, I am exhausted,* I said to Rashid. I said that the years I wanted to know about and finally understand were years that had been bent, slapped around, shoved, and kicked aside by silence and lies.

My memories, I told Rashid, were like FBI documents with days and months blacked out over here, years over there. I may have never repressed them, but neither have I processed them, or even thought about them much in the last five, ten, or twenty years. How to attach faces now, hands, and responsibility to the fast snatches of images that exploded in my head, exploded and then evaporated? How to do that and still sound credible?

The way abuse works is by erasing the horror of itself even as it is occurring. But not only the horror, also its victim, her opinions, what she sees and feels.

(*You know you want this, say you want this, say it now, bitch, comin' up in here lookin' like that, what the fuck you expected, say you need it*—I need it—*say you want it*—I want it—*say you love it*—I love it—*say who fuckin' pussy is this*—yours, it's yours—.)

For months these conversations kicked inside my head, stomped inside it, until finally they became the only sounds I could hear, and when that happened, when I could hear no other sounds, I began to see things. I began to see my life, not as it was right then, but my life as it had once been. My old life once more became a movie, but this time with only one scene playing over and over on my apartment walls, on subway windows, on the streets where I walked. I kept seeing my once-upon-a-time self. I was thirteen. Eventually I told Rashid.

When I turned thirteen and got my working papers, I had a series of part-time jobs, and at those jobs, at nearly every one, there were all these men, and they were older than me, usually by ten, but often fifteen, twenty years.

I said to Rashid that this was when things began to happen in horrible succession. I explained that unlike so many other survivors I was reading about, my home was a safe place. For me, it was the world outside that brimmed with violence and danger, and although I knew this, I would venture willingly into it, into all the cracks and crevices New York City had to offer. You could find me there, in those cracks and crevices.

This is why I think maybe it wasn't abuse. (This part was whispered.) *I remember that I liked it, not the sex, and not the touching, but being wanted, it validated me somehow. It made me feel special. It made me feel human. Being wanted. It made me feel human.*

When I said this, I felt ready to put the whole matter away, to accept the blame, and to move on, but Rashid argued with me. He was the first one to say it, to confirm that what I had experienced was abuse. *Because,* he said,

You were a child, asha. That's what made it abusive. You were a child.

Rashid was soft when he said this, but he was firm, convinced of his position. I was not, however, and I told him so.

I can't remember that, I said quickly, but after, when Rashid got up and went to the bathroom, I closed my eyes and tried to see what he told me he could see: me as a little girl. I did not succeed, though, not then, and when he returned I told him once more,

I can't remember being a little girl. By the time I was twelve I felt all the way grown. I swear I did. I'm not exaggerating. If you saw me then, Rashid, you would understand. The way my body was, the things I thought about.

Rashid stared into my words, he frowned into them, and this was when he asked me to describe how it was in the fullest possible detail so that we could look at that time together. Perhaps together, he explained, we could understand those days in a brand-new way. Rashid said this, but I was too afraid. I knew that in the moment I said to him all of what I remembered, I would forever be another woman in his eyes, and would he still love me?

Can we do this later? I asked, but Rashid did not agree. He reminded me that I was the one who said you cannot hide from your past, your life, yourself. And when he did this, when he reminded me of my own words, I began to tell him things, slowly. Over many months and many visits, I revealed the years between thirteen and eighteen. Initially I was vague, offering only minutia, but Rashid pushed and finally there was an afternoon when I told him specifics.

I told him that although the faces may have changed, and the places may have also, some things could always be counted on to remain the same: the pulling, and grabbing, and pinching, and slapping, and all those dirty words, and all those bad names, the leering, the propositions. But of all of those men, I told Rashid, there was one who stood out. There was one man who was so mean I thought about him regularly, unlike the others. The others I blocked out. I don't even remember most of their names, but that man, I thought about him again and again. He would come to me in the night and kick me out of my dreams. He would come to me in the day, when I had been wrapped in the arms of another man. A man who was safe. He would come to me and when he did, he could make good men seem bad, frightening, and dirty. I told Rashid this. *I've had flashbacks of the man and I've had nightmares of him. Sometimes it didn't look like him. Sometimes his face was different, but I was never fooled. I always knew who it was,* I told Rashid, and then I said the man's name out loud. I said it and watched the surprise push out over his face.

You said that man had been your boyfriend, asha, and you said he was beautiful!

He was, I explained, *not my boyfriend, but beautiful, my God, he was so beautiful.*

I told Rashid how he looked: tall and brown, an indigenous man from the mighty Sioux nation, an unrecognized prince with a braid down his back, three black belts to his credit, a wide, fast laugh, and $200-a-day cocaine habit.

That was how I saw him when we first met.

The man told me I was the prettiest girl he had ever seen. The man told me that love was what mattered, not age, not the fact that he was twenty-eight, and I was fourteen. *So what?* he had said to me, I can still hear him saying it.

He worked in a movie theater as a security guard. The theater also employed my girlfriend, and sometimes I would fill in for her, and sometimes I would go there and just hang out with her. That was how I met him, I explained.

I told Rashid about the evening I went down to the movie theater a few weeks after I'd met him. I told how the man said he wanted to talk to me, and on the inside I smiled. On the inside I felt special, and I followed him down the stairs into the staff lounge, and once again he whispered in my ear that age did not matter. And once again, I had believed him. I had wanted to believe him. I believed him even when he backed me up against a locker, even when he began undoing the buttons on my blouse, and even when I said slow down and he did not slow down, not then, and not when when I said it again, *Slow down! Please!*

I said I was not ready, even though, I explained to Rashid, I thought I was ready. But being ready was not the point. The point was that I wanted the man to love me and to respect me, and all my life I had been taught that saying no was how you got those things: love and respect.

I told Rashid how it was such a conscious decision on my part, when I said *Slow down*. I remembered clearly thinking that if I told him to slow down what would happen was that first, he would slow down, then he would think I was a nice girl, a good girl. After that he would rebutton my blouse, and smooth my hair. After that, maybe not that night, but perhaps the next, he would bring me flowers, and then he would fall in love with me, and then I would begin to exist in the world as a relevant person, a person who was necessary because I was a person who was loved. But not just loved, loved by *him*. This is what was important, because he was grown, he was twenty-eight, and he was beautiful. I was fourteen and wrong. That's how I felt back then. Twelve and wrong. Thirteen and wrong. Fourteen and wrong. Alive and wrong and wrong and wrong.

And I wanted to be set right, just once, just that time, in front of him. He was beautiful, I was wrong. This was what I was thinking all at once, in the same moment, and that was why I said it to him, *Slow down, I'm not ready.* I said it to him, and then I prepared myself to be loved, caressed, and respected.

But that did not happen. The man did not say he loved me. He said I was nothing but a fucking tease, an ugly bitch, a cunt. He slapped me in my face, and then he punched the locker I was leaning against, and the locker reeled backwards and then forwards again, and it knocked me in my head, and the pain rushed through me, it buckled me, it broke down the air in me, and for a second I could not see, but then I could. My sight returned.

The first thing I saw after the darkness was the man raising up his fist again, and I didn't know if he would hit me or the locker, but either way I knew I would lose, and that was when I ducked my head and began to run. I headed toward the stairs and my shoe twisted, it nearly came off my foot, but it did not, and I ran and fell up those stairs out onto Eighth Avenue and behind me the man was screaming, *You nasty fucking cunt, you think you so fucking cute, you ain't that fucking cute!!* And then a cab came, and I got in, and it sped away. But that was not the ugly part of the story I told Rashid.

The ugly part of the story didn't come until weeks and weeks later, when it was summertime and I ran into the man in Central Park. We were both alone. We had not seen each other since the night at the movie theater, but when he greeted me, he smiled and did not mention the violence between us. He told me I looked beautiful and that he would like to sit with me. Would I sit with him? he asked, Would I smoke a joint with him? he asked.

And now, today, I know myself well enough to understand that there is a part of me who always wants to make what is ugly somehow beautiful. This is part of why I write, I suspect, why I love art, all expressions of it. But I didn't know this then, on that late summer afternoon, that the reason I went with him was to make a new memory, a memory I could enjoy, a memory that could sustain me. On that late summer afternoon, what I knew was that I was feeling mesmerized by everything, the easy heat on my skin, his beauty, the fact that he still wanted me, and the possibility of what sweetness we could create together.

And it was me. I was the one who said it. I said it of my own volition, *Yes*, I said to him. *Sure, let's go,* I said, and we walked over to someplace in the park more remote, and we sat and we smoked, and in the distance we could hear a radio playing, and we moved against the music and his arm was around my shoulder, and now he is telling me I am beautiful, and somehow I am actually feeling it, beautiful, I mean, and for a time the whole world is no more than me and the music and the summer air, and our bodies close, warm and soft. And the whole world is the sun, which is leaving the sky with all of this grace and dignity, and the moon, which is huge and gold, and the man's arm around my shoulder, holding me.

But suddenly it is his weight I feel, his weight overcoming mine, suddenly this becomes the world. And then the music disappears and the moon disappears and even the season, the summertime disappears, and of course I do as well. I disappear. It will not be the last time. It was not the first.

What remained after I was gone was a body that was no longer my own, and he kissed it, the man did. He kissed it with an anger so complete that he actually was biting the top of the lip that was once mine. And my ex-body did not scream or squirm. It did not move until the man slapped the inside of one of the thighs as a signal that it was time to open up, and the body that once was, but is no longer mine, opened up, the legs did anyway, and the man got between them.

The man undid his pants and he tried to push into my ex-body, but he found that it was hard to do with all the clothes between us, and that was when he dropped his arm across the face on my ex-body. His hand was across its eyes, his elbow poked in its ear. He balanced himself. He said, *I'm gonna fuck the living shit out of you.*

And for however long he was in the body that was, but is no longer mine, that was indeed what he tried to do. That was what he nearly accomplished in doing; not fucking the shit out of, but fucking the life, nearly up out of that body in the breaking night of summertime, behind dried bushes, on dying grass. And when we parted that night, there was no good-bye, no I'll call you, no see you later. When we parted that night, I would never see him again.

And I would never learn to call this rape or abuse because I went with him willingly, I got high with him willingly, and I did not scream, not once. But there would be many things I did learn from him, from that time. *I see it now,* I told Rashid.

I learned how saying no can get you beat. I learned how my age didn't matter because nothing about me mattered. I learned how I could just abandon my body if things got ugly, that my body could handle it while I sat on ceilings, on pieces of the sky, and watched the whole disgusting thing.

Waiters, bartenders, drug dealers, musicians, chefs, actors, students, camp counselors, and managers, when the workday ended, and the ties came loose, there wasn't a fucking difference between them. Beyond all other lessons that I would learn, that was what being a teenager in New York City in the 1980s would teach me most of all.

∼

Trying to heal, I would discover, was not a steady process, not by any stretch of the imagination. Despite all the candles I burned, specific candles for each day of the week, despite the early morning meditations, journal writing, prayers, and healing exercises from one of the thirty or so books about childhood sexual abuse I bought, things just did not move in a predictable straight line from awful to bad to manageable to good.

I could wake up in the morning feeling hopeful, filling myself with all the light of the early sun, and by afternoon I could be wondering what was the fastest way to kill myself. There were so many possible triggers for absolute despair: a news item about an abused child, a man on the street who said something to me too aggressively, a friend touching me on the leg in a way that seemed familiar, ancient, and terrible. Part of the problem was my approach to getting well. I didn't know this then.

I have always been impatient, since I was a small girl, a toddler rushing from one toy to the next, from one corner of the room to the next. As I grew up, I became notorious for my ability to consistently overlook the most vital part of an instruction manual, or trying to carry too many things at once. Inevitably I would drop one or two items, and sometimes they would break, and sometimes they wouldn't break, but always I made a mess.

What I did when I first began trying to heal was skip right to the end of my books where there were all these testimonials of women who were survivors. I ignored all the parts in the beginning about definitions of abuse, and the steps I should take, and instead I absorbed the most wrenching stories of women who had been sliced down the middle by fathers, step-fathers, uncles, and brothers. They had spent their childhoods being hustled between emergency rooms and social workers.

None of the stories I read sounded like mine. That was what helped to confirm me in my own mind as a liar, a fraud. The eight or nine testimonials I read and reread became for a time the only definitions that I accepted of sexual abuse. They were testimonies of incest or of a single abuser: an uncle, a family friend, molesting a child over and over. My story didn't fit. My story had many characters in it, there were many men, and generally, once they did it the first time, they left me alone. Generally.

There was something else. I had good parents, loving parents, parents who gave my sister and me everything they could. The only time I ever had to go to the hospital was when I had put things down my own throat, and when I thought about that, how I had sent my own self to the hospital, I thought about how I must have been a fraud. And the idea of me being, on top of everything else, a liar as well was more than I could stand, and it sent me out into the world looking for blood.

I felt I had to find a telltale trail of blood, and if not that, then at least a nasty wound, a swollen discolored bruise, a scab, anything. Anything. But that never happened. I didn't find it, and I know on some level I'm writing this all down now because I'm sure there must be other women out in the world looking for blood like I was looking for blood, and they won't find it like I didn't find it, but they should know they are not frauds. I was not a fraud.

I was a young woman whose memories came rushing in at a

time when phrases like false memory syndrome were thrown around, when therapists were accused of implanting ideas in their clients' heads and this and only *this* was the reason for the apparent epidemic of sexual abuse in our society. It would be a long time before I felt strong enough to defend myself against these sentiments.

And it would be even longer before I learned how Sigmund Freud's original work documented sexual abuse in the lives of his female patients. I learned that when he did release his findings, there was a huge social backlash. I learned that if the society was to believe its women, what then would they have to conclude about their men, the ones who ran the government and the banks and the businesses? Freud retracted his findings. But I didn't know about all of this back those nights when I'd lock myself in my bedroom and rock and grind and let the sweat and snot run down my face and forget to breathe and try to convince myself there was a reason for me to live. Even if I couldn't remember it right then. There was a reason.

No, back then, I had not read anything by Freud. I had read books by Nabakov. I had read *Lolita,* and I saw myself there, squatting between the pages, a nasty girl, a freak.

Of course there was a simple logic to this: If I blamed myself for everything, as I had all my life, then I could seek revenge on myself. The men were gone but I was here, and I could attack myself as I always had. I knew how to self-destruct, with drugs and alcohol, overdoses, unequal and abusive relationships, food. I could make anything a weapon. I could wield anything against myself. There was a certain satisfaction in it. It took so long for me to change, longer than all of my friends who got high and did stupid dangerous teenage things; I did them well into my twenties. I might still be doing them if I hadn't met Rashid, if we hadn't been involved.

When I became involved with Rashid, I still drank even though alcohol was beginning to make me sick. One beer and I would want to pass out. I still smoked cigarettes and weed even though I *hated* being high and my throat was sore all the time. I still had uneven friendships.

It's not that I think Rashid is or was some sort of miracle worker. My husband is a man, flesh, blood, and flawed like every one of us. But Rashid was willing to read the books and Rashid was willing to stifle his temper when I threw misdirected fits of rage. And he was, more than anyone else, in the line of fire, but he did not move. And there were times that I knew he did need to get away from me. He won't admit it, but I know it's true. And this is where the prison actually served our relationship; it forced us to be apart, and during that time, that was probably a good thing. I hate to say it but the separation probably saved us. No one can live in the throes of that sort of intensity and anger for too long, and when things would become very terrible between us, the phone would cut off, or the visit would end, and we'd have to each go back into our own separate corners. I slunk into mine.

There was one other thing. Rashid and I could not have sex. At that time, we were not married, which meant we could not have conjugal visits. And as painful as it seemed then—we used to go on and on about the need to be together—the reality was that I didn't need to be having a physical relationship with anybody. The reality was that I was not emotionally equipped to handle it.

We had little to distract us from the issue at hand, and when

I would begin disintegrating into all of my own fears, night-mares, and insecurities, Rashid would say to me again and again,

You were a child, asha.

(I didn't feel like one so was I really one?)

What if it was your daughter?

(Don't say that to me. I don't like you to say that to me.)

What if you were your own daughter?

(Please stop.)

Imagine that.

(No.)

Just once.

(I can't!)

Please!

And after he pushed me for what seemed like the thou-sandth time, I tried. I covered my face with my hands and tried to conjure up a picture of me as my own daughter, a little girl, a teenager. I tried it a second and then a third time and then a fourth time, and then a fifth, and finally, finally an image moved into uneasy focus. If I blinked, it would disappear. She would disappear. I knew this and so I concentrated, and as I did, something inside me began to shift.

Once I read a book that said *What if you came home one night and found everything had been ransacked, some stuff was missing, some stuff was broken? What if a window was smashed, a door kicked in? You would know that you'd been robbed, even if there was no thief right then, in the vicinity.* At last I came to under-stand that that's how it was with abuse. That even without the trail of blood, there was evidence, and the evidence was me, my house, with its drawers roughly pulled open and rifled through, its floors littered everywhere with shards of glass and rusted nails. My house with valuables missing.

And when I could see this, I knew that it could never have been simply teenaged angst, that it wasn't just puberty that had stormed through my house and made me crazy. The damage was too devastating, too complete. And because it was, there would be no storybook life like the one my parents had dreamed for me and worked so hard to achieve. And no matter what, I could not change or forget or drug or drink or sex or analyze or even love my own history away, and the best I could ever, ever do was rebuild. And this made me profoundly sad for a time.

For a time all I thought about was what would a never-molested asha look like? That question stuttered my movements, my breath, and my sight. Would I have gotten a Bachelor's Degree in four years instead of fourteen? Would I have walked away from the drugs? Would I be able to drive? Would I like my body? Would I have been able to say no to the food, the drugs, the alcohol, the abusive men, and all the years of hysteria and depression? Would I never have had the persistent and crippling sense that I was dirty, a whore, a funky bitch, not good enough, an undesirable?

I asked those questions of a friend one afternoon. She was also a survivor, and we were having lunch in a Thai restaurant in Brooklyn. I was whispering and crying and she was holding my hand, and she leaned across the small table, across the food, her face was inches from my face, and she told me that I was not a liar, or crazy or wrong or broken. She told me I was also not perfect. But I could stand, she said. I could walk, she said. I could write and I could tell the truth. And I could understand.

She said I could understand that in the end I would not be defined by my experiences. I would be defined by what I chose to do with my experiences, if I was open and willing, and uncompromising and honest.

one day my soul sat down and rested

i come from people who prefer silence, who believe that refusing to give a name to a thing will send it away. They have lived like this, and they have survived, my people, and they have built their families and done their work, and found their joys. My own parents raised up, both of them did, out of childhoods that had been punctured by poverty, death, and departures, and they had rarely spoken about what had been lost to them, and what had been taken, what it was they mourned, and what it was in the long and hidden hours of their own lives that they cried for.

I was always different in this particular regard. Saying what I feel is something that I have done since I first learned how to speak. I have never been able to contain my feelings, although there were many times I wished I could have. Without some process for verbal expression, I know I will go insane, or else I will die. This is something I know for certain.

Silence already tried to kill me, not once, but many times. That was what I thought about immediately when I considered the possibility of never saying a word to anyone about the abuse. And not saying a word was absolutely a very real option. When the memories came I was tempted toward silence. The last thing I wanted to do was to alienate myself further from anyone; the abuse had already marked me, I felt. It had already made me an interloper inside my own self, and I didn't want people to see that. I didn't want my friends to see me as someone different now, or Rashid to see me as someone damaged now, or my family to see me as someone dirty, or worse, as someone indiscreet.

But finally I did reject it, the silence, because I knew the way it operated. I knew that whatever pain did not come, distinct and terrible, from out of my mouth would find an escape route in some other place. That was its history with me, the silence's. For fifteen years it had crept out through my hands every time I reached for a spliff laced with angel dust, a vial of cocaine, a glass pipe filled to its blackened rim with freebase, a tab of acid and a hit of mescaline, a taste of heroin, and two Quaaludes washed down with beer, speed taken with shots of tequila chased with Dos Equis, glasses of vodka tonics, Budweiser, Riunite, Canei Rosé, and Champale, that were followed later by pizza with double extra cheese, Oreos, a pint of ice cream, and then two fingers down my throat. I could swallow anything, put anything inside myself, there was no limit, except passing out, which I did, many times, in bars, on streetcorners, in unfamiliar apartments, and in the arms of men whose names and faces are lost to me now.

For years, as a teenager and young woman, I had lived like that, on the outside of my own body, watching my soul wander through cities and men and unequal friendships and drugs and food, and jobs I hated, and by the time I got to Rashid, and found myself facing him with this big, terrible thing that I did not understand and could not control, I was tired, so incredibly tired, that I had to tell him so. I could not hide it.

I told Rashid that I understood that I was no longer somebody's small precious little girl, and that I could no longer be held in my mother's soft, comforting lap. I could no longer have someone come in and rescue me out of my bad dreams. I had to rescue myself, I knew that, but I asked Rashid if he would please be a member of my team, and he agreed, and this was most clearly when we defined ourselves as that, a team, and afterwards we would never go back to being completely separate people; afterwards there would be this burn we shared, you can see it on him, and you can see it on me. On each of us the burn appears different, but somehow you know it came from the very same fire.

But on that day when I asked Rashid for his help, when we were sitting in the visiting room where I could see a small piece of the sky and I was wishing I could fly into it, I looked at my lover and thought for sure he would reject me. I thought he would say no, he could not help me, or that he would say nothing at all, but what he said was, *Come here to me, asha.*

He said, *I will not leave you, asha,* and he said that whoever I had once been did not scare or sicken him, and in the end his love for me would be bigger than all of my scars added up together. And this last thing, he did not just say it to me, he promised it to me, and when he did that my soul sat down for the first time that I can ever remember, it sat down and it rested. It rested for hours that became days that became weeks that became months that became years and when it rose from that rest, it was smiling, she was smiling, my soul was. She smiled for hours and hours and hours, she would not stop smiling, and even today, you can see, she has still not stopped smiling.

red

*t*he irony of it all would hit me later, that there in a prison, suspended beyond time, caught in the small space behind Plexiglas, I would begin to feel free. I never did go to therapy for the abuse. I read books and talked with friends, but for the better part of the first three years of our relationship, it was mostly Rashid who worked with me. I went to him regularly to confess and to cry. I went to him stumbling and I went to him shrieking.

And Rashid stood firm. He studied the same books I studied. He became an expert on a topic that he had never thought about before except in passing. I cannot think of one wrong turn he made during that time. Not one moment of insensitivity. Not one word misstated. Not one look askance. Not one accusation that *perhaps I really wanted to, didn't fight hard enough, basically just gave my pussy away, deserved whatever I got because I wore my skirts too short, my lipstick too bright, should have known when I went there and danced like that and spoke like this, and besides everybody knew what kind of girl I was anyway, so what? What?* Rashid never said to me the things other men have said to me. Still say to me.

And it was because of how kind and smart and loving he was that it seemed particularly unfair that when the feelings of freedom began to stir, they only began to stir inside of me. Not inside of us. Not inside of Rashid and me together. Just me. As I was beginning to feel in control of my body, my lover was spending his days waiting in line to be frisked, strip-searched, passed through metal detectors, trying to get on the phone, and hoping for a piece of mail from me that sometimes came. That sometimes didn't.

Nevertheless I could not contain myself and cautiously I began having a conversation with Rashid about what I was thinking. I told him that something strange but also wonderful was happening. I told him that for the first time in a long time, I wasn't plowing through my days thinking only of the abuse. That hours and almost whole days went by without me feeling that it had me snatched up by the back of my neck.

I feel so strong these days, I told Rashid. *I almost feel normal,* I told him. *I feel in control of myself. I never felt in control of myself like this before. Like I have some power over my own needs. Like I have some power over my own body. I listen when my girlfriends talk about the men they meet, and I don't quite have the same sense of sovereignty over myself that they do, but I'm not where I was before.*

And Rashid said that this was wonderful, that it was the news he wanted to hear, but he didn't understand all the ramifications of my new feelings. He did not understand because I had not yet articulated them to him. I had not said how the initial rush of love which had carried me over our daily difficulties had begun to sputter. And although my feelings for him had not diminished, I was starting to see my life as though it was a child's brand-new coloring book: I was all thick dark outlines. Nothing was filled in or differentiated by hue.

I was in no hurry to say these things to a man I felt had just helped to save my life. And I was in no hurry to revisit a topic we'd discussed when we first fell in love—monogamy. When we first became a couple I had said to Rashid that I just didn't see how a woman could be monogamous with a man when he was doing big time in prison. We had gone back and forth, back and forth, and begrudgingly Rashid had acquiesed to my point of view. But aside from a few dates, there had never been much reason for the issue to come up. Not until now. Now that I felt free.

Despite my hesitation at raising the matter, at no point was I blind to or unmindful of what was happening inside me. Out of loyalty and guilt, I tried to shove my feelings away. I spoke, hypothetically, with a few women I knew from the van rides upstate. I hoped that I would find out from them how they balanced their love for their husbands with their own desires and need for attention. But much to my shock, every one of the women I talked to had *friends*. Every one of them said it was necessary. They need their *friends*. To keep them sane, they said. To ease the loneliness, they said, and to add a little color and spice to the bland soup of prison life. I was just like those women.

Like them, I knew I needed more colors in my life but I could not imagine where to find them. I suspected that the magical box of sixty-four colored Crayola crayons had been deemed illegal and was now also incarcerated. Sienna and burnt orange, canary and magenta. I thought they had been buried somewhere in the deepest, most solitary part of the jail where I could not access them. A part with no visiting rooms and no visitors, no windows and no views.

From a place behind my eyes I did try to see a world inside the prison that pulsed with the fullness of living and possibility, but I could not find it. Yet I did not just give up hope. There in the visiting room, in Rashid's arms, I would attempt to do what had always worked before. Once I could simply escape us both into my imagination—we would just leave, set up residence there, but now even my mind was failing us. On one visit, two visits, three visits, and four, we were stopped by the prison which had barricaded every door to our possible other worlds. If we were lucky, we'd get a fast glimpse of a better place, but as soon as I was away from Rashid, I'd forget the little bit of promise we had seen together. I told Rashid everything I was feeling. He looked at me helplessly. I looked at the floor.

If only Rashid could have colored me in! Draw in the lines, my soul used to plead during each of my twice-weekly sojourns upstate. I used to plead through my glances, and I used to plead through my touches. I used to plead through the switch of my hips as I walked toward the door at the end of my visit: *Follow me, Rashid, come home with me now. If you loved me, I know that you would find a way.*

How to survive? This became the overriding question in my life. I would wake up plotting. Everything I bought, everything I did, everyone I befriended was a tool designed to keep me alive, living, able to see at least some of the world's beauty because I could not live without color. Not live and be productive. Not live and be at peace. These were the matters that began to jumble and distort and compromise every other possible discussion Rashid and I could have had.

I told him that I loved him, but I loved myself as well. I said I had no choice but to pull on every resource I'd ever had, every bit of mother's wisdom, every healing book, every scripture, and to mold them into sinew and begin to move through the world refusing to capitulate to what the prison would have made me: old before I was thirty, bitter, brittle and breaking.

I begged, and I borrowed, I cajoled, and I conjured. In the end I found I had somehow cobbled together my own box of crayons, worn but still useful. Feeling inspired, I decided to reject any limitation at all. I set out to collect watercolors, pastels, acrylics, oils, and chalks. I painted my world with poetry, music and dance, politics and new places. And Rashid just watched me from behind that wall and gun tower. *You're just doing your thing,* he'd say to me as I began to travel more and more. More and more I began to find reasons to be away from the prison. More and more I'd forget to make decisions *with* him. I'd just say, when he called, that I was off to this women's conference, that campus to do a poetry reading. I began to cancel dates I had with him. I wrote letters less frequently.

At a conference one summer I met a woman who was getting ready to start a nonprofit organization. She needed a partner, she told me, someone who could codirect the program with her. She asked me if I was interested, I said I was, and in one unbelievable month I told Rashid about the offer, said I was going to accept it, and that in thirty days I was moving to San Francisco where the organization was based.

San Francisco? Rashid exclaimed, but after the surprise wore off, he just said, *Okay, baby, if it's going to make you happy. Okay.* He asked only that we make a schedule of when I would come to see him. *Sure,* I agreed, not knowing that the job would keep me on the road at least two weeks out of every month. I was able to travel back to New York City fairly regularly on business, but my visits to the prison still became infrequent. Even when I moved back to New York, as I eventually did, I never would go back into them as often as before.

I imposed a distance, not so much between myself and Rashid, but between myself and repression. I told Rashid that because what he and I shared was bounded by the rules of the jail, I had resolved to open up the other parts of my life. *I have to,* I said to him. I said to Rashid that it had not been enough embracing new cities, new jobs. Sometimes I needed love, I told him, other love, I told him, other men. Not scores of them, or even several of them. But a few of them.

Whenever Rashid and I talked about having an open relationship, he would tell me he could not understand how I could love him and yet go out with even one other man. I, on the other hand, marveled at the fact that it hadn't been hundreds of other men. Though even hundreds of men would never be an adequate measure against the intensity of the isolation.

I need them, I told him. Human contact, to feel desired, to walk through a neighborhood holding someone's hand. *I need that.* Not every day, I told Rashid, but some days. *I don't seek anyone out,* I said, *but I cannot resist loving the ones who seem to just appear before me, open and pure.*

It wasn't a question of sex, although sex was sometimes a part of the picture with a few of the men I met. It was going out to movies and dinner and poetry readings and clubs that I longed for and that made me feel almost normal. I explained to Rashid that the times I shared with those men often pulled me through the days when the days angrily threatened to leave me like a hostage, blindfolded and bound to bars and locks, razor wires and guards. Those men held me when I needed it, and some even loved me when I needed it. Then too, one nearly broke me.

There had been one man with whom I'd been friends for a long time. And from that safe place, as friends, we'd shared secrets and problems and sadness and dreams. And although he never said it, I knew that man saw my life like it was some tragic film. I knew he saw me like the heroine in the film, the woman tied to the tracks. And I did nothing to deny that vision. I waited to be rescued, and one night after a long-distance disagreement with Rashid, the man came to me. He united my hands and he untied my feet.

And for that one moment, we were like our favorite celluloid heroes. Of course it was only for that moment, since it is only in the movies where everything is scripted: the conversations, emotions. We had forgotten that we were alive, real lives. Neither one of us was prepared for the work that it would take to write our own story. Our plot ideas conflicted.

The man didn't want me to love Rashid anymore, and I wanted the man to love me only in the limited spaces I provided, just there, nowhere else. What happened next was not surprising. We became an ending before we had become much of a beginning. Our relationship, the whole of it, the romance and the friendship, ended after a long week of fighting. Still, we had created this havoc that laid itself for a long, long time, like some huge, heavy tarpaulin, across my life and across his life, and also across Rashid's life.

I suppose there must always be the risk of feelings expanding wildly beyond your initial agreement with someone. This is what Rashid always says he fears most, that what begins as a lunch date ends up as me falling in love, ends as me leaving him. He fears emotions as no longer cool, crafted things, but emotions as weapons, as crude shanks, rusty and dangerous.

When he told this to me one afternoon, I said I understood. I said, *Rashid, you are so right*. But it was something I knew only after I had been stabbed by those renegade emotions, and now my scars are a witness. Rashid's scars are a witness, yet his wounds seem uglier, more raw, infected perhaps. Some of them have never stopped bleeding no matter how much pressure or first aid we have applied. When he kisses me now, sometimes I can feel the place where another man's touch slit open the sweet taste between us. I try but cannot avoid what has become our truth: Rashid's tongue is lined with the unmistakable salt of blood.

We kiss and both of us drip red.

≈

During this time there was one visit where Rashid held my face in his hands and we were so close I thought he was breathing for me. I could not sense where my air stopped and his began.

On that visit, he said I came to him in his dreams. He whispered that to me, his mouth directly upon my ear. Even still I could not hear him. *Say it again?* I asked.

We are together, away from the prison, back in Guyana, up in the countryside.

Rashid began explaining to me. He said when he dreamt of me, that was how most of the dreams began.

But I have other dreams sometimes, and those other dreams are the ones that tell me.

Tell you what? I asked.

I have dreams that tell me about you. They tell me when you go out, when you've met some man.

I don't understand.

I'm saying to you that my dreams tell me everything you do. I wake up and even though I can't remember details, I know. I have this horrible feeling in my stomach. That's how I can always call you the day after you've gone out with someone and say to you I know what you did last night. Or say to you if someone called you. You kept asking me, How do you always know, Rashid? *You thought I had you followed but I don't have the money to have you followed. I just have dreams. I've always had dreams. I didn't always pay attention to them. I should have. Maybe I wouldn't be here. Maybe a lot of things. But the point is that now I'm different. Now I pay attention. Now I don't miss a thing. Never.*

≈

Rashid and I had many disagreements over how restrictive our relationship should be. I felt that I should not live by the same sexually repressive rules which had been forced upon him. I felt that the difference between me and many other women in my situation was that I was completely honest about my feelings and needs. Most of the women I knew did not discuss this topic with their partners. Finally, I felt most emphatically that if the situation were reversed, no one would have even expected Rashid to wait around for me, let alone be monogamous.

Those were the positions I presented to Rashid again and again. I presented them and felt justified. But I presented them and then turned away quickly because after all, there was nothing I could say to stop the pain from wildly crisscrossing his beautiful face, crisscrossing it and kicking it, slapping it and distorting it. There was nothing I could say when Rashid would whisper to me, as he always did during these discussions,

How would you feel, asha? If I was somehow involving myself with other women, how would you feel?

≈

One afternoon the visiting room was unusually quiet, and I'm
sure that was part of what made Rashid and me also quiet. We
had decided to try things his way. We had agreed, for a least a
time, to forget the idea of an open relationship, and for the
first part of the visit we nearly did not fuss or argue or even
talk. We did not need to talk, to sort things out the way we had
before this agreement. Now the way we touched was itself
conversation. The way we touched said everything. But as the
day pushed forward, I began to miss the sound of my lover's
voice, which is why I did eventually ask him,

Are you okay, honey?

Yes. I'm fine. Are you comfortable? Rashid responded because
I was lying against him, as much as I could, with him in his
chair on one side of the table and me in mine on the other side
of it.

I am, I said, and really did mean it. I was very comfortable
and it seemed Rashid was as well, which was why I did not
understand when he stabbed into the quiet with a bayonet of
words.

So did they deserve you?

What are you talking about? I asked. I nearly exclaimed it,
although I knew exactly what he was talking about.

*When you spent time with some other man. Did he, did any of
them, deserve you? I mean it's true that you might have deserved
attention, you might have deserved a night out, but what about
them? Did they deserve you and your energy and your time? Had
they worked to be with you, to earn a place in your heart?*

I did not answer. I did not tell Rashid that it was not a
question I had ever really considered: What I deserved. What I
didn't deserve.

Rashid leapt at my silence. He said,

You don't have an answer? Never mind, then. I'll just tell you what I think.

I think you deserve a man who isn't afraid of you, and who isn't afraid of everything that brought you pain, and who will face that pain with you, no matter how ugly it is. You deserve a man who knows how to make you laugh, asha.

You deserve a man who will tell you when you're wrong, and who will listen when you tell him he's wrong, and a man who is going to be just as open as you are, and just as free with his thoughts as you are, and just as willing to struggle with himself as you are. And a man who wants to make the world a better place as much as you want to make it a better place.

You deserve a man who loves your poems, and who wants to hear you read them again and again and again. You deserve a man who's not afraid of being passionate, and who loves to kiss all of you, not just your mouth, but all down your back, on the bottom of your feet. You deserve a man who wants to cook for you, and raise babies with you, and be old and tired with you. And I think that these things are the least of what you deserve.

What you deserve is a man who will always protect you. Protect you with his life if he has to.

asha, Rashid said—said like it was the one true thing he would ever say—*asha, that's me.*

what there is to lose

*P*art of what allowed Rashid and me to lurch toward closure on the issue of monogamy was that I finally made an admission. It was as much an admission to myself as it was to him. It was an admission which allowed me to release some of the confusion and fear which came dragging in behind me when I fell in love with a man in prison.

I confessed to Rashid that on most days I woke up to the scent of the same old and persistent insecurity. It informed many of the decisions I made, and the fights Rashid and I had. And it had been there since we first fell in love. It was the insecurity with the sour breath and the mean, crooked trickster's laugh. Devoid of sympathy or softness, it would drop its hard judgments across my face and there was no escape. *asha,* it would say to me, *you know the man only loves you out of limited choices.*

Throughout the course of our relationship, people have warned me about the manipulative, dishonest, even abusive ways of prisoners. I have heard a warehouse full of stories about convicts who siphon off all of their wives' money for sneakers, food packages, and cartons of cigarettes. The end of the story is always the same: the man gets released and after a short time, leaves his wife with a broken spirit and an empty bank account. And in each story another woman is somehow involved.

It's not that I don't appreciate the concern of the people who love me. It's that their willingness to cluster all prisoners into one simplistic stereotype never leaves any space for Rashid's humanity. The prisoner, the man I have come to know and love, doesn't demand things from me. He doesn't order or even ask me to bring him money or food and clothing packages. We negotiate all aspects of our relationship, usually based more on my needs than his. Rashid's behavior defies all the stereotypes I have heard, but these questions remain, nevertheless. Most of the time I am the one who is doing the asking.

I think the greatest gift that can be given to someone you love is to give them the gift to see themselves as you see them. All your flaws in full recession, or at least perspective. I told Rashid that in the end, whether or not he proved to be an honorable man, I knew that was the gift he tried to give to me nearly every day that I had been with him. I told Rashid it was my own shortcomings which stood between his offering and my receiving. If only he knew, I said, how I wished I could see the asha he told me he could see.

Rashid sees a confident, funny, brilliant woman. He sees a desirable woman. He sees a woman other men would give their right arm to be with. He sees absolute beauty, unfailing intelligence, and an indescribable radiance.

I see the new pimple on my face.

I see every book I have not had the discipline to write. I see the fifteen pounds I always want to lose. I see the extra mile I do not run, the dessert I do not avoid, and the sugar I am addicted to. I see all the times I feel awkward and cannot think of anything intelligent to say. I see my hair out of place.

I see the men I loved who didn't love me back. I see the desperate need I had to convince them all that I was worthy of one more date, one more call, one more touch, one more anything. I see every mistake I ever made, every time I was unfair, every time I lost my temper, and every time I didn't try hard enough. I haven't quite figured out how to see radiance through all of that dark, cloudy shit.

I told Rashid that this was why sometimes I wanted to go out with other men. Sometimes, I wanted to go out with men who chose me from a sea of women. I told Rashid that, despite everything, sometimes it was so hard to believe that he *really* loved me. Sure, he thinks he does, I would tell myself, but just wait until he sees all the fine women gliding across the streets of Brooklyn. All the women who are everything I am not. The ones who have voices which never crack or sound hurried or strained. The ones who have only been touched by men who loved them, or at least respected them. The ones who have always respected themselves. The ones who went to the prom, or had a high school sweetheart. Those women.

The women with the skin that looks like sweet mocha-cream. The ones with the tight unblemished bodies which never, ever weigh in at more than one hundred and twenty-five pounds. The ones who have never been addicted, afflicted, in need of therapy or a personal library of self-help books.

I assured Rashid that I was not a series of various neuroses, but I was hardly the picture of womanish confidence that he envisioned. I explained to my lover that I tried and tried to push back the doubts and affirm the beauty. I said to him that I knew I was blessed to have him in my life. But no matter what I knew, there were times when I had nothing to fill the space his absence created in my life. *That's when I vacillate about us,* I said.

≈

You have to understand, my girlfriend said to me once, when a brother is locked down, naturally he's going to feel insecure. You really have to see this, asha. You're out here running around the country, halfway around the globe and back, meeting all kinds of people. He knows other men are going to approach you and even interest you. And he knows he can't really compete with that. So, of course he's going to trip when it seems like you're trying to look all sexy. Plus he's Muslim and he's the Imam. And that makes you *automatically the Imam's wife. Which of course is its own kind of drama.*

I was complaining to my girlfriend about a fight Rashid and I had over a dress I'd worn. We had faced the abuse, the question of monogamy, and my choice to travel to the prison less frequently. But now, when for the first time in a long time we finally had the prospect of some peace, Rashid had begun picking on me about my clothes being too short, too tight, too American. *What happened to all those long, flowing African dresses you used to wear?* Rashid would ask over and over, as he pulled at my skirt in a futile attempt to drop the hemline.

People and styles change, I said, as Rashid made faces and hissed.

That thing is too damn short and you know it. Why do you always let all these men you don't know see so much of you?

The dress, in my eyes, was quite an average, unsexy business dress. It came to just above my knee. On other occasions I had conceded that I had been immodest, but I refused to give in on this one. I felt he was unjustified. But after I'd talked with my girlfriend and she raised the possibility of Rashid being insecure, I did not do what I would have normally done. I did not send him a mean letter and tell him to relax. I sent no mail for few days and instead just reflected on her point.

I thought about how Rashid always exuded such an air of self-assurance that I had never considered the notion that he could also be insecure. My own doubts were so encompassing, I never took the time to wonder about his doubts. But the truth is that most men in prison have at least one *Dear John* letter shoved in their lockers. I knew Rashid had one shoved into his.

For both parties, then, prison romance is at best a calculated risk. Those of us who are in this odd and unnatural place learn to soothe ourselves with the kind of negative reasoning that says, Well, on the outside, relationships don't necessarily work out. Even marriages in America end in divorce 50 percent of the time, so what have we got to lose?

Love and insecurity are an ill-fated couple. Yet there they are, together all the time, rolling around in the bed, accusing and then assuaging, and then accusing each other again and again.

My thing was running. Always had been. Probably always will be. Get out while you can still recognize yourself, that's my philosophy. Get out before you hate somebody you used to love. I've picked fights with Rashid not conscious of what I was doing until after the damage was done. And I could fight about anything, the tone of his voice, religion, a simple request, an answer that came too slowly. I could make anything seem bad enough to prove that we really ought not be together.

No one needs a psychology degree to figure this out. There was something inside me that hoped Rashid would decide that I was not worth it. I was too argumentative, too difficult. If

Rashid got mad or tired of my rantings, maybe he would tell me to leave. If he told me to leave, maybe he would decide I should never come back. If I never come back, maybe the pain will subside, the loneliness.

Rashid, believe me, I said when we were discussing insecurities, *I am not a woman who likes to play games. I go back and forth because I am scared,* I told him. *I understand,* Rashid said. He said it and he held me. *And I also have this problem,* I continued. *I could never be strong enough to leave of my own volition. I'm a woman in love. In love and in trouble, my mother would say.*

power

for two years before Rashid and I became a couple, I had volunteered, taught, and read poetry at cultural events and programs in the prisons. Once or twice word would come back to me that one or another of the prisoners had a complaint about me. Sometimes it was because I used a curse word in a poem, other times it was because one of them thought my pants were too tight. But most often when I did a program in the prison, I received extended standing ovations and repeated requests to return. The majority of brothers I met were very kind to me, warm and respectful.

As soon as Rashid and I went public about our romance, all of that changed.

Suddenly who I was became a point of contention with many prisoners: the way I dressed (too suggestive); the way I spoke (too profane); the way I offered myself to the world (too friendly). Worst of all, my name was deliberately evaporated. I became known suddenly and solely as "Rashid's woman."

Prison is a macho place. Security. Us against them. Pumping iron. Mean faces. From the superintendent's office to the incoming convict, it's all about might makes right. Physical or mental, everything in prison is a power play; who can out-lift, out-survive, and out-will whom. And within all this, there we are, the loyal women. We stand by our men. We bring up baby, along with cigarettes, junk food, and expensive sneakers. We women, we do it all despite weather and welfare.

As I write, I read pieces of this story to friends of mine. Many of them comment, correctly so, on how brave Rashid is, having parts of his life discussed so publically and graphically.

You have all the power here, a few of them said. *You being the writer. You're like God,* some said.

Still others pushed the issue further. Others proclaimed I had all the power in every part of our relationship. The life or death of our love rested precariously in my hands. It was me, I was told. I brought freedom and outside light to Rashid's dark, dank, caged situation.

There are months, so many months that I can no longer count them, that the phone bill comes in, five hundred, six, sometimes eight hundred dollars. Within the pages of the bill are lines and lines detailing the costs of the collect calls I accept. Collect calls are the only way Rashid can reach me. And me? I take $20 cab rides, run, cancel appointments, end dates abruptly in order to make it home in time to accept a call he and I had previously arranged.

I don't know why you two just don't cut this phone business down, Rashid's father said to me the one time we were all together at the facility for a big prisoner-and-family picnic day. I was annoyed by the statement, but not surprised. Others have said the same type of thing to me. They have said it as though our relationship didn't suffer enough communication lapses and distances. But people have tried to make me feel guilty for needing to connect with my husband.

There were years I took lesser-paying jobs because they allowed me the flexibility to visit Rashid during the week, which was something we both preferred since the weekdays were less crowded. When I go shopping now, I often buy clothes only if I think they will meet the dress code imposed on visitors by the prison. And later, after Rashid and I got married and were granted conjugal visits, there were times when I missed important events because they conflicted with the dates that the prison had scheduled for us to be together. Sometimes there were events which could have possibly propelled my career, but I couldn't imagine what would make me cancel time with Rashid. Besides, if I tried to get a postponement, it could have been months before we were rescheduled.

All of those daily realities made me wonder what my life would look like if I really was that God some people had determined me to be. What would my life look like if I was even a mere shadow of that God? What if I *could* write into existence all I ever wanted, or even all I ever needed? My words as magic wands. My words, not as a metaphor for power, but as the thing itself. My words as a synonym for creation.

Those people are, I suppose, so certain in their analysis that I have all the power, because I can come and go as I please without being frisked or shackled—as if my legs moving, walking, up and out are not connected to my heart, beating, feeling, needing. And my heart is always right there, trapped in that prison, no matter where my legs may find the strength to carry me. Nobody mentions that.

Others who have felt compelled to throw their two cents into the debate have commented that Rashid's ability to virtually command me upstate, that my changing the ways of my life in order to allow for prison rules and restrictions, gives him all the power. Rashid, a man who is told when, where, and how he can see and touch me, is constructed as a man with all the power.

In the meantime, and on numerous occasions, the phone company has blocked Rashid's collect calls not because I have paid my bill late, but because they *think* I might pay it late. It's their policy, the long-distance carrier has explained to me. If they think the bill is getting too high, they'll just cut me off. They'll cut me off without notice. They cut me off without repercussion. They'll cut me off no matter how lonely I am, no matter how much I may need to hear Rashid's voice, and no matter how much he may need to hear mine. Never mind that I haven't ever paid a bill late, no matter how costly it was.

One day recently, a guard terminated a couple's visit because he felt their six-year-old-child made too much noise. We, each wife and husband, each girlfriend and boyfriend, watched with disbelief as the couple was being separated. We held our own partner more tightly, and cursed the police under our breath, and wished terrible things on him, and then we thanked God it wasn't us being dragged apart two hours early. Of course next time it could be us.

We knew an unjust or incorrect accusation from a guard, a lie from a guard, could determine a prisoner and his wife's ability to see, touch, or smile at each other. A computer-generated restriction from a phone company could stop our ability to even talk. And those things could happen no matter who has the power.

That is what I tell people when they offer me their theories. The phone company can beat my ass, it can reduce me to long sobs of frustration and loneliness, but I'll keep coming back, crawling, money in hand, bruised, maybe broken in places, but I'll always keep begging.

Regardless of what anyone else might believe, I know there are no simple answers, no one-line solutions to this question of prison love and its relationship to power. I say there are no simple answers to most things in life, though often I've tried hard to reduce them down, choose sides quickly, and then maintain my positions forever and ever. For Rashid and me, however, this is not an option. In prison, there is no place for the simplified, the redacted, the easy way out.

To hold on to ourselves and our sanity, what Rashid and I must do is master the art of being fluid. We can neither make things too complicated nor too simple. We must be great negotiators, willing to compromise without selling ourselves short. We are unnetted trapeze artists, Rashid and I, balancing when to fight with police with when to ignore them, when to spend money for another collect call with when to fold our emotions into a package we put away for another time. A better time. A different time. A later time. Or else a time after that.

marytr

*t*here was a time after we were married when Rashid sent me a letter detailing some of the restrictions which were being imposed upon incarcerated Muslims. Access to the room they used as the mosque was suddenly restricted, which in turn affected the ability of the men to pray together and to fellowship. Then, suddenly, the Department of Corrections wanted to control the food choices for Muslims on their holy day celebrations (food that the men pay for themselves). Rights were being chipped away at slowly but consistently, leaving the men in an odd predicament. The rights that they had lost were too small to provoke any widespread uproar, yet if things continued along the path they were headed, soon they would have no rights at all.

Rashid closed his letter to me with a quote which is reported to have come from the Prophet Muhammed. It read,

Whoever of you sees an evil action, let him change it with his hand; and if he is not able to do so, then with his tongue; and if he is not able to do so, then with his heart—and that is the weakest of faith.

I wrote a fast and thoughtless response to Rashid which thankfully I never did wind up mailing. Out of concern for his safety, I'd told him to leave all these issues alone, but I tore up my letter because if my baby didn't take a position, then who would take a position? The media and politicians have constructed prisoners as people who have adopted religion as a con game, and perhaps some have. Some prisoners may use religion as a tool to get a few small privileges. But most of the prisoners I have encountered are deeply committed, sincere believers. I mean, wouldn't you be, surrounded by noise, anger, violence, depression, and steel, wouldn't you give your life over to a greater power?

Rashid may be the most sincere man I have ever known. And he has always been religious. As a child in Guyana, he was a deeply committed, Sunday-school-going, Bible-quoting Christian. The years between Christianity and Orthodox Islam saw him embrace the Five Percent Nation, Masonry, and the Nation of Islam. His beliefs now, the longest held of all of them, seem to me a very natural progression.

And so the question was, how could I do it? How could I say to him, *Baby, please, hold back . . . let someone else do it . . . can't you just pray and be silent . . .* Me, a woman who lives all of her life in public, on the page, asking her partner to restrict his expression. I knew I wasn't being fair, but I didn't know what I was supposed to do. Was I supposed to willingly sacrifice the man I love to prove my own sociopolitical commitment? Was I supposed to be ashamed that I'm a woman who just wants her man to come home, and not in a body bag?

When he helps another inmate file a grievance or get their legal work together, when he refuses to allow the prison to discard his humanity, Rashid takes his whole life in hands, all the love that is in him, all that is right and just, all that is imperfect and all that is scared, he takes the father in him, the son, the brother, and the partner in him, he takes all that makes him rise and think and pray and dance and scream and make love and struggle, he takes everything and risks it, with one sentence, one challenge, one legal document, one disagreement.

For those who want to know, this is the real story of prison life. Not color televisions or weight rooms. Those things exist only to distract inmates.

After everything I've seen, the only story of prisons that I am able to write is the story of the intimidation and the fear that I live in every day of our life. If we argue with a guard in the visiting room, if there's some kind of policy change, if another prisoner gets attacked and needs assistance, what will it mean? Will it mean Rashid will be set up with drugs? Will a guard try to set him up to be killed? These things are not products of my imagination. These are things that have happened to us. And they are documented. They are known. They are everyday business. They are simply not stuff the six o'clock news ever chooses to cover.

I began a new letter to Rashid first by telling him that I didn't believe that I was made of whatever it took to be married to a martyr. History instructs us that they kill people who rose up and challenge the status quo. But as I was writing, I started thinking about how I believe in transformation behind the wall. How I believe in it and support it. I started thinking about George Jackson. And I started thinking about Angela Davis. And, it was in the middle of those thoughts that the memorial service for Dr. Betty Shabazz came on.

I set the letter aside and watched Myrlie Evers-Williams and Coretta Scott King as they stood there together, shaking at the podium, desperate to explain what it was to have lost their husbands to the movement. Coretta Scott King said that as she watched Medgar Evers shot down in 1963, she wondered if this would one day be her fate. She said that when, in 1965, she saw Malcolm X killed in front of his pregnant wife and four children, she knew that her turn was coming around the corner. Mrs. King said that she, Myrlie, and Betty were sisters, albeit sisters pulled into existence by tragedy.

I knew I never wanted to be part of that kind of sisterhood. That was the next line of the letter I wrote to Rashid, though I did not write it without a measure of guilt. It was not that I supposed my partner to be a Malcolm X, but like so many people I knew who had committed crimes and who now wanted to turn their lives around, Rashid embraced only the highest of moral positions. So much of his early life was handed over, he said more than once, to these base emotions: greed, lust, and selfishness. Today Rashid lives for others. Today he lives for God.

Sitting in my room that day watching the memorial service, trying to write that letter, and feeling the full weight of prison-imposed fears, I thought about all of the years I'd spent as a student organizer. I thought of all the protests, and I thought of my work with Black Panthers who were now political prisoners. I thought about my unwaivering positions on issues of self-determination, women's rights, and economic justice. And then, shocked, I wondered, could it be possible that in the end all I really wanted was the man I loved to be at home with me where I could see him and touch him, build and create with him? And at home, where I at least had the chance at trying to protect him.

Whatever changes Rashid was going to make in this world, I decided I had to be there alongside him. Not me as a distant witness, and not me on the other end of a horrible phone call. If ever there comes a time that we've got to go out, then we've got to go out together.

And that's what I finally wrote to Rashid as a response to his letter. If there's business to be handled, I said, either figure out how we're going handle it together or else leave it alone. Period. That's it. End of discussion.

time

*P*rison toys with time, teases its meaning, confuses those of us trapped and defined by the fourth dimension. During visits and phone calls, minutes and hours disappear within a single greedy swallow. Whatever else may need to be said—and there is always something else which needs to be said—must be postponed, put on the back burner, minimized, or forgotten.

Waiting for the court to rule, *just to rule,* on an appeal which could free Rashid, is horrifically long, dragged out like his homecoming. The years stretched out, yawned, took their own sweet time to pass. They went on vacation, those years, and left me staring at calendars hoping that eventually they would indeed return and get the job of bringing Rashid home to me finally done.

Every time I looked up, there was always more time ahead of us than there was time behind us. As I write this, there are six more years left on Rashid's sentence, and that's just the time between today and the parole board where Rashid could get hit with more time. He's got life on the end of his bid, so there's no guarantee of anything.

I get lost when I think about what could happen in my life in the next six years, what has already happened in the past six years. I am not the same woman I was a half decade ago, not even close.

Six years ago, I was married to another man; the idea of falling in love with a man in prison had never even crossed my mind. Six years ago I spent weekends in clubs and bars. I smoked cigarettes and I drank alcohol regularly. Six years ago, the idea of getting my own book of poetry published by someone was a fantasy. I was barely willing to read my poems publicly. Six years ago I hadn't finished college, and didn't know if I was ever going to finish college. Six years ago the only emotions I could access regularly were anger and pain.

Six years ago I wouldn't have liked the woman I am today. I would have thought I was boring.

The woman I am today prefers to stay home, is still attracted to, but doesn't want to get caught up in, "the mix." Today I am a vegetarian who eats organic foods. Today I have finished my Bachelor's degree and am nearly done with my Master's. I am a published poet now, and have read my work before audiences in New York State prisons and before audiences in London, England. I don't go to clubs and rarely to parties. Today I set achievable goals, concentrate on them, and complete them in realistic time frames. Today I time-manage and write daily. I do affirmations. I meditate. I run. When people ask, how did you finish school finally, stop smoking, get published? I tell them, *Slowly.* I tell them about discipline and focus and isolating yourself into your own dreams and hopes. I tell them about struggling to never live in reaction to my fears.

In six years, I asked Rashid once, *what will happen to me? I think about how I could have six new lives in that time. How am I supposed to stay here with you? How realistic is this relationship? How do other women do this time?*

I looked to him for answers that I knew and he knew he would never have. Our relationship is strictly trial-and-error. Or trial by error. And I cannot imagine how I will make it. And I cannot imagine how I won't.

~

You know what the difference between you and me is?

Rashid began speaking, his voice low and our faces huddled close in the visiting room. We always do whatever we can to resist the imposing *clang clang* sounds of vending machines, and the booming of police shouting, *Visiting room to central!!! Open!! clickclick . . . hmmmm! bang!*

The electronic steel door, which is controlled by a man pushing a button behind a two-way mirror, slammed open and a guard passed through. The door slammed shut quickly with all the same noise and drama, but we managed to resist the cacophony. We even managed to resist the sensory-depriving, noncolors of the walls, numbered tables, and hard plastic chairs. We choose the rich, defiant tones and texture of our flesh, eyes, and humanity instead.

The difference between you and me is that with every day that passes, you see a little bit of your life slip away. Every day is one day further away from your dreams not being met. One more day without your family intact, without the babies you want to have, without your partner being home with you, without having any real home at all.

But every day that goes by for me is one day closer to having what I've always wanted: a beautiful woman I can cherish and be with, a family, a good job, being in the street with people who I can work with to make things better and stop all of these kids from coming into these jails.

He was right and I was silent, saddened, and scared by the truth. Once again, our needs have collided and then exploded upon impact. Nobody is ever right and nobody is ever wrong. We are left there, trapped between nowhere and nothing.

Powerless, we are, as though we have been strapped in and forced to ride the passenger seat of our own lives.

And time, she moves, a dancer to her own drum, elusive as the wind, unconcerned, uncommitted, unsympathetic, and unavoidable.

between god and religion
and rashid and me

*a*ll of our struggles are not big, prison-imposed struggles. Some of them are regular, everyday sort of troubles, troubles that other couples, couples who have never even seen a prison, have. And while neither of us like to fight, when we argue over these every-couple sort of things, we know it is a blessing. Rashid and I crave normalcy even when it comes on the edge of an argument.

Islam, Rashid's religion, would be one of those everyday sort of battles, and it followed us as a source of dissension within our relationship. I never could reconcile myself with what I understood as its patriarchal doctrine. From the very start of our affair, Rashid began the process of attempting to convert me. He denies this. He denied it then, and he denies it now, but I know better.

During the two years in which our relationship was strictly platonic, never once did Islam creep into our conversations. And back then, we would have these long, winding discussions about politics and social issues. We were, all of us, the prisoners and the students, open, personal, and fairly unrestrained. Oddly, however, Islam was never mentioned.

Once Rashid and I shifted into romance, everything changed, and changed without warning. I became a sudden and unwilling audience for long passages from the Qur'an and even longer rationales on parts of the scripture which I found particularly disturbing. In one section I read the manner and circumstance under which a man may beat his wife. Rashid said he would never hit me. I told him I was not comforted by that fact.

In the first place, I would usually argue, *I already have a wonderful relationship with God.*

And if you ask me, I said, *I think religion generally gets in the way of a good relationship with God.*

I told Rashid that I found no space for myself, my woman self, in Islam. Everything I saw in the religion taught me how I was supposed to be a good daughter, or else a good wife, but there was so much womanness in me between those two definitions. In the Islam I see, I can't find space for the asha who has all of this history. This history that's shaped me. This history that's hurt me.

In Islam, there's no space to forget for a moment, about being responsible to a husband or child or parent, and just go get my nails done, or go for a run, or wander aimlessly one afternoon, or buy a dress I don't need, or dance, or kick it with my girls, or laugh raucously, or gossip a little, or do a million other imperfect or else immodest things that I do to get through some of my days. I can't find the space to exist in all of the full sensuality of my regular expression.

The religion, I told Rashid, would harness me back from my own spirit. That scares me, I told him.

I told him that, *In Islam, I never find the room to fall apart. Never room to take a day off. There's always some neat answer to problems, and I just don't see life like that. Things aren't that neat, and sometimes the only right response to a problem is to fall apart. And believe me, when the man you love is in prison, sometimes, you have to fall apart.*

Maybe you see something I don't see. Maybe there is room in the religion that I just can't find. Maybe there are things that I don't understand. But until I do, I have to leave it alone.

I continued by explaining that the religion was too severe for me, that I did not understand the love of God based on this long set of rules. I explained that I needed a God who loved me for doing my best, even when my best isn't very good. And, I explained, I did not want to be in a religion where men cannot shake my hand or hug me unless we're married.

I believe in human contact, I say. *I don't think touching has to all be considered sexual.*

In this society, it is, Rashid argues.

But we can't let something negative define our behavior. We have to define our behavior. I'm going to keep hugging people and holding hands, and if I have to say a thousand times I only mean this platonically until they get it, fine.

But what happens if you hug the wrong man? Rashid asked.

Over the years, this is how we go, back and forth, point and counterpoint. I do not understand him on this issue, and he does not understand me. After a few rounds, we always agree to disagree until something brings the issue back onto the table. Of course, something always does.

But as much as I want to, I cannot simply dismiss Islam out of hand, because Rashid says that his religion saved his life. And religion beyond simply a belief in God, which he has always had, but religion as a code for living, a structure, a strict set of rituals, a chart directing him through every minute of every day. Islam, with all its specificity, was and continues to be Rashid's primary catalyst for transformation.

Beyond precise moral instruction, Islam determines methods and times of daily prayer, how to kneel. It tells you how to dress, what to eat, how to manage your money, and how to resolve conflicts. It tells you how to romance someone, how to make love, and how to raise your babies. It demands complete obedience, and when you have done wrong, it does not shirk from meting out punishment.

Islam, then, is the parent Rashid never had. This is what I have finally come to understand. In his life, it is an entity that has been as instructive and consistent as my own mother and father have been in my life. When there is no one else to love him, there is Allah, his Messenger and his message.

When there is no one else to love me, there is my mother and father, their particular morality, advice, and admonishments. And it is these which have always embraced me and kept me in a way Rashid's people never did. Not when he was a boy, and not now, as he is a man.

Once I asked Rashid about birthday celebrations he had when he was child, and celebrations he's had since he's been in here. He says he cannot remember ever getting even a card from his mom or dad.

Maybe when I was boy. I can't remember though. Nothing since I've been here. No card from them. Nothing.

Rashid waits a moment and recalls, *My mother used to send packages after she left and went to the States. But I don't know if they came because it was my birthday. I think she just sent packages sometimes. It's fine though. Really,* Rashid adds, but I do not believe him.

≈

There was a woman we would see regularly in the visiting room. She and her husband were Muslims, you could tell by looking at them. He wore his *kufe,* and she was always in the full *hijab.* She became the bain of my existence, that woman, always there as a reminder about how short and fitted my dresses and suits were. Rashid has never and would never ask me to be covered from head to toe, though I know if I did so he would not complain. I could tell by the way he'd sometimes comment on her outfits. I could tell by the way he'd comment on mine. Finally I fought back.

I argued to Rashid how the couple had two small children and on most visits the woman would bring them along with her. On most visits, too, she had some kind of intense sexual interaction with her husband, sometimes full intercourse right there, while her children looked on.

Rashid and I had no idea how they were able to carry this off. Most couples hug too long and suddenly there was some guard standing over them just waiting for a hand to slip into a forbidden zone. But those two, they really could go at it with no apparent repercussions every time they were together. I'm not accusing anyone of anything, but it was strange for any couple to have such freedom.

That curiosity aside, what was really relevant to me was not *how* they were able to do it, since they weren't friends or associates of ours. What was relevant was that they were Muslim, and as Muslims, a religion certainly defined by modesty, they were the height of immodesty.

Look at them, honey, I whispered one day. *She may dress the part, but look how she acts!*

It's true, I may wear dresses above the knee, but I never behave like she does! I would never let you behave the way she allows her hus-band to behave! I feel quite righteous in this moment as I motion toward the couple carrying on in front of their children. I sit back in my seat. I grin.

Rashid grins too. He grins and then says, *I think we ought never to compare ourselves to the worst of all possible examples. I think we ought always to compare ourselves to the best the world has to offer.*

Rashid looks at me. He waits for an answer, a rebuttal perhaps, and for several miserable seconds I search my brain for one. Finally I say quickly,

Nevertheless, my point remains. You should judge me by my actions, not my clothes.

Rashid opens his mouth to respond, but I kiss him instead and tell him I am hungry. *Let's get some popcorn,* I say, standing up to walk over to the vending machines, satisfied to have had the last word.

He smiles at me, aware of what I am doing. The conversation is over, the disagreement unresolved, but at least we are laughing.

All right, Rashid says. *Come on,* he says, and takes my hand. And when he does this, I look at him. This is a man who liberates, not oppresses, me. He liberates my thoughts and ideas, all of who I am.

Yes, my spirit is liberated, even here behind a wall, a razor-wire fence, and four electronically locked doors. Here with Rashid, I have never felt so open, so free, or for that matter, and by extension, never so close to God.

sight

*W*e lived on a land with no borders, in a city with no center, down a street with no name, in a house with no walls, where there were windows with no bars.

We were free in this place, Rashid, we were free. And can you remember? How the days moved with no time, how the years did not stunt us? How we shared language with no words, how our silence was the singing that made the sky begin to dance? Remember this, beloved? The way the sky danced bold and the way the sky danced wide? The way she seduced us and the way she seduced herself with her beckoning arms and her winding hips? The way she claimed her space and the way she leapt and then changed colors?

This was a dream, but it was not a night dream. It was a day dream, and it came to me one afternoon in the middle of Manhattan where I was walking, wondering if Rashid had ever walked here, on this exact street. I was wondering if he had ever walked here and felt the sun laying down on the back of his neck, the way I was, right then, feeling it lay down on the back of mine, and if he did walk here and feel that, did the sound of the cars and the people stop for him the way they had stopped for me? I could not hear them. I could not even see them.

I could only see Rashid. I could only see Rashid and me. I could only see Rashid and me, and the land with no borders, and the sky above the land, the sky that danced.

One day when were together in the visiting room I asked Rashid if he ever saw this place, the one from my dreams.

It was so vivid, I said to him. *I think you had to have seen it. I* pulled Rashid near to me. I said I thought he had to have seen it even from this place, this cage with no air, beneath a sky with no stars.

Rashid leaned back in his chair and then he closed his eyes and then he nodded his head slowly.

Yes, he says to me, *yes, asha, I saw it. I can still see the place when I look out the window, when I look just past the doors. I can see it every day.*

a wedding at the prison

*e*ver since you and Rashid became
involved, he's wanted to marry you. In Islam, there's no such
thing as boyfriend and girlfriend! *He has argued this point to you
from the very beginning, but you never did find it very compelling.
What you have found compelling was how good the man has loved
you for almost five years. What you have found compelling was the
history the two of you have created, and that if you got married, you
could at last be alone with him. One morning, swept up in a whirl-
wind of desire, love, and hope for the future, you tell Rashid,* Yes,
yes, yes. *You tell him you can handle being married to a man in
prison.*

*Two months later you are standing outside your apartment
building, waiting for the prison van. You are alone and it is five
minutes to five on a Tuesday morning. It is springtime, but it is cold.
You remember how it was the first time you married. You remember
that first the sedan picked you up from your parents' house, and
later, an Excalibur drove you and your groom off to a five-star hotel
where you stayed until it was time to fly off to your honeymoon in the
Greek Islands. You wonder how things could have changed so radically. You feel very confused in that moment as you look down the
road to see if the prison van is coming yet.*

*Freddie, the van driver, had said for you to be outside at ten min-
utes before five. He is late and now you are panicking. What if he
forgets you, you wonder, even though he has never once forgotten
you? Is the lateness an omen? This thought comes to you but you do
not hold on to it. You snap it up, and then throw it aside. Another
five minutes passes, and then finally, finally, you see the van coming,*

tumbling down the street as it always tumbles down the street: as though it is too heavy, as though it will tip over.

You are wearing jeans and Freddie notices this when he gets out of the van to open your door. You getting married in that? *he asks.* No, *you say.* There's a dress in my bag, *you say.*

You climb into the van. The only seat available, except for two in the tight back, is the center one in the first row. You have never seen the van so crowded. Not before. Not since. You climb over a woman in the first row who barely moves to let you in. Right in front of you, in the place on the floor where your feet should go, is a huge box, a package you're sure that someone is leaving for a prisoner. In order to fit, you must put your feet up on the package. Your knees press into your chest, and you wonder how you are going to make this long ride. With all the stops in between, it will be nearly four hours from door to door.

You arrive at the prison, it is just past nine. The women and children line up to be processed. You do not. You have brought a dress and you want to change into it, fix your makeup, try to look pretty. You wait until the women have been cleared to enter the prison so that you won't be interrupted while you are in the ladies' room, and for about five minutes, you are not bothered. Then, as you are putting on mascara, someone begins to pound manically on the door. You think there's an emergency, a fire, and you rush to unlock the door, but before you get to it, you hear the voice of a woman.

The woman on the other side yells Yo! Somebody in there? *And from the tone in her voice, you realize she just wants to use the toilet. You cannot believe it! You are annoyed that she didn't just use the other bathroom. That bathroom is exactly like the one you're using, except it says* MEN *on the door instead of* WOMEN. *But since men rarely visit anyone in prison, that bathroom is regularly used by women. You yell through the closed door. You say to the woman that you'll be out in a minute, but of course you don't mean exactly a minute. You mean as fast as possible, which you thought was understood, but after a minute goes by, a minute to nearly the exact second, she begins pounding again. This time, you yank open the door and curse her out. You are ready to fight. You indicate this, that you have no problem stepping to your business. You don't know what you look like when you say this but the woman seems to take you seriously. She backs up, mutters, walks away from you, and suddenly you are embarrassed at what this must look like to the police who is standing at the desk to the left of you, waiting to process you.*

Back in the bathroom, you remember getting dressed for your first wedding. You remember how your mother taped a piece of lapis to you. It was something blue, she said, but also for good energy. You remember your sister helping you on with your dress, and the photographer who captured that moment, the zipping up of the dress, on film. It's all important, *your mother had said, about even these most intimate pictures being taken.* You'll cherish this one day, *she'd said. If only she knew.*

But she doesn't know. You have only told her that there is man, a man who is in prison. You have not told her you're marrying him. You have not told her how much you love him. You are scared to tell her and even more scared to tell your father. You have always been the kind of daughter who suspected that there wasn't much room to make mistakes. Even if there was room, surely it must be gone now, considering all the trouble you caused as a teenager and young adult. You don't want to lose your parents. You decide to tell them nothing. And there is a price for that decision. It is your wedding day, and you cannot remember ever feeling quite so lonely, quite so isolated. You emerge from the bathroom.

You hand the police your visitor form. He knows you are getting married. Sure you want to do this? *he asks. You do not answer.*

You resent all the intrusions into your feelings by people you don't know, people who don't know you. When you requested permission to get married, there was the counselor who talked with you about Rashid, his crime and his sentence.

Mr. Rashid has a sentence of twenty years to life for the crime of murder in the second degree. Are you aware of this? (Yes.) This means he will not come up for parole until after he has served a sentence of twenty years. Are you aware of this? (Yes.) Mr. Rashid can only apply for family reunion visits after you've been married for ninety days. After the ninety days, Albany will decide if you're eligible. If you're eligible, you'll be placed on a list to participate. Are you aware of this? (Yes.)

The counselor had gone on in this way, as though Rashid wasn't sitting there at the table, and finally when he finished and left, you had exploded. You were mad because you thought he was disrespectful to Rashid by not addressing the both of you during his monologue. You were mad because the man had made it seem as though Rashid was not there, and you didn't need one other thing to make it seem as though Rashid was not there. You began to go on, to become consumed by your anger, but Rashid had interrupted you. First he kissed you and then he said, Don't pay that shit no mind, baby. He's just doing his job. The important thing is that we're getting married. *You agreed. But you were still mad that day.*

And you are mad right now, weeks and weeks later, as the police asks you that question, You sure you want to do this? *You want to ask him why he cares what you do, but instead you grimace. You go through the metal detector. You head into the visiting room.*

In the visiting room the officer assigns you to a special table, one over in the corner and almost hidden behind a pole. He is trying to be nice, to afford you a modicum of privacy. You understand this. You even appreciate the effort, but it does not replace how exposed you feel. You continue to frown as you sit there, waiting for Rashid to arrive.

You look at your watch. Rashid is taking longer than normal to get into the visiting room. Frustration begins to build inside of you. You begin to think about running out of the prison with no explanation. If you do that and if later Rashid calls to ask what happened, you could say he should have been more timely if he really *wanted to marry you. You could put the blame on him. You are thinking this as that question—*Are you sure you want to marry him?*—twirls around your head, twirls and jumps and yells and snickers. You begin having a heated argument in your head:*

What kind of stupid question is that, anyway? *You silently demand this, hands on hips, neck going, mouth twisted.* Who can ever be sure of anything? *You continue, even as you know that the argument you are earnestly trying to erect is poor, at best.*

Another part of you starts rattling on about lots of things that you are sure of during your life. It says that there are lots of things you're sure of right now. Getting married just isn't one of them. The argument is over. No use fighting with the truth. You crumble into defeat but not before cursing the police who asked you the question. You will the tears back behind your eyes, and then you read the list you have made in your head. This is what you're sure of:

That you and Rashid need to be alone. Not just for sex, although sex is a big part of it. There are these other important things the two of you have never shared. You have never cooked for Rashid and you want to. You want to make him one of his favorite dishes: vegetable curry and roti (he'll have to handle the roti), banana bread, avocado salad with your special secret dressing, honey-pineapple chicken, or else blueberry pancakes, vegetarian sausage, and plantains for brunch. This is what you're sure of. This is what you know.

You know you want to touch Rashid, your skin against his skin,

*an hour-long massage. You want to rub his feet, give him a long hot
bath, wash his hair, oil it, oil him, let him relax in your arms, let
him sleep there while you watch him, this is what you're sure of on
the morning of your marriage. You decide it is enough, and you tell
Rashid you're ready when he finally walks into the room.*

*He walks in wearing a white shirt, a shirt you've never seen
before. He's carrying a bouquet of yellow tissue-paper flowers.* Here,
baby, *he says, smile wide as a river.* My friend made these for you.
Every bride ought to have a bouquet. Especially my bride.
That's why I took a little long to get down here. The stupid
police didn't want to let these in. But I figured you didn't have
family here, you didn't have friends or a cake or nothing, so
you should at least have flowers. Here baby, *Rashid says again.*
Take them.

*And you do, you take them. You think they are stunning, more
beautiful than the roses from your first wedding, the wedding where
your whole family came, the wedding with the expensive printed
invitations and four-tiered cake and the open premium bar and the
Tattinger Brut de Brut and the live band and your bridesmaids in
peach dresses and ushers in tuxedos, and the woman from the Ethi-
cal Culture Society who officiated, and the honeymoon in Greece,
and all that love and support and hope and approval everywhere,
flowing from everyone. Who could have predicted, who could have
known, that just ten years later, you'd be here in a prison, with no
one, no one there except Rashid and his friend, a man called Natural. Natural, who was also a prisoner, had agreed to witness, to be
the best man.*

*He's there, Rashid's friend, when you pick up the flowers, the yel-
low paper ones. He's there when you try not to cry, but the paper
flowers are the evidence of all you have and all you do not have. They
are why you cannot help yourself. You begin to weep, to sob, and*

Rashid doesn't understand. He thinks it is him. Did I do something, baby? *he implores.*

It is not him, but you do not say this. You only cry. You cry when the Imam comes and asks both of you if you are truly ready to honor a marriage contract. You cry when you exchange vows in the corner of the visiting room over the sound of change clanging in the vending machine and the argument someone is having over who gets the last microwaveable chicken sandwich.

You cry when the guard says, Okay, folks. Visiting room is closed. *You cry as you leave and Rashid thinks it's him.* Baby, do you think you made a mistake? *he asks, desperate and terrified. You don't think that.* Of course not, *you say. But you say it with less conviction than you should have said it. You know this, but you leave.*

It is night, your first night as Rashid's wife, but you don't feel any different, since everything looks the same. When you left the prison, the midday spring sun was no brighter than usual. The night moon is no more round, no more golden now. When you get back to New York City, you do what you could do on any night of your life. You meet a girlfriend. She takes you out. You eat a big fattening Italian dinner and a huge dessert. All that food makes you feel sick but you eat anyway. You eat and eat. You get drunk from the food. You tell your friend it's time to go home. You go home. You get in bed. You are alone. It is your wedding night. You are alone. You hope you will dream of Rashid. At least that. At least. You think of him and you think of him. You slide your hand down your body, play with your nipples, open your legs. You imagine Rashid is kissing you. You love the way Rashid kisses you. You can almost feel his tongue, lips, and teeth mixing with your tongue, lips, and teeth. You slip you fingers inside yourself. You raise your hips, and now you can almost see him entering you, first slow, long, and then fast, faster. He is in you. He is you. You can call up the sensation, Rashid in you, Rashid as you. You feel yourself begin to rise in yourself. You hold your breath for several seconds and then you start to come. You come hard. You say Rashid's name out loud. You say it the way you know you will say it when he does finally make love to you. That day will get here. This is what you are praying for and imagining, right before you fall asleep. You fall asleep, but you do not dream.

eve

*e*xactly ninety days after the wedding, Rashid applied to the Department of Corrections in Albany for eligibility in the family reunion program. Four weeks later we were given a date. We were informed that we would have our first conjugal visit, what we call a trailer, a reference to the housing on the prison compound in which we will be staying, in less than a month. I received a letter of instruction from the prison, and my life divided into a list of *can do's* and *cannot do's*.

The letter told me that I could bring in my own sheets and towels. What I could not do was bring in my own sheets and towels if they were orange, blue, white, gray, or green.

I could bring in my own shampoo and conditioner, lotion, makeup, and soap. I could not bring in my own shampoo and conditioner, lotion, makeup, and soap if they contained any sort of alcohol.

I could bring in my own packaged foods. I could not bring in my own packaged foods if they were packaged in glass or under pressure, if they contained poppy seeds or alcohol.

The instructions went on and on, and then they went on some more, and for three weeks I spent hundred of dollars on regulation sheets and towels and toiletries and bags and bags of food. I shopped for seasonings I hadn't had to buy in years: salt, black pepper, sugar. By the time I was done, I had bought a near truck-load of packaged foods (*Just in case,* I told Rashid.

We're not going to have to time to eat, he responded. *Not that stuff anyway,* he giggled.)

Shampoo bottles, lotions, conditioners, and hair gels, I meticulously read labels that before I'd never even noticed. Every one that I picked up seemed to have alcohol in it. I became overwhelmed with anxiety. I paced aisles in drugstores. I confronted store managers and demanded to know *exactly* why they don't carry nonalcoholic toiletries.

Eventually I found a hodgepodge of what I needed and I began to pack. It was still several days before the visit. I packed. I waited. And it was during that period of waiting, when I only had time to imagine what our trailer visit would be like, that it dawned on me: Rashid was about to see me naked for the first time. Upon that realization, I had a full-blown anxiety attack. My skin got blotchy. My breath tightened. Sitting down, my heart rate stayed above one hundred and twenty beats per minute. I was a mess.

I began to roll back through all of the years and all of the visits I'd spent disguised by pretty dresses, mascara, lipstick, and eyeliner. Now Rashid would wake up with me. As is. Raw. But the idea of us being alone got even scarier. It got even worse.

We were going to make love. We were going to make love after four years that had been marked by small kisses that we held in our mouths and stored behind our teeth. We used to hold our breath, trying to make those kisses last. And they did, those kisses lasted so long, they became our sex, whole and complete.

And now I was terrified. I was terrified that I would never be able to live up to the sexy fantasies that we shared with each other in letters, on the phone. Now that it was time to move past the small caresses Rashid and I had become used to, I was scared I wouldn't know where to go or how to get there. Making love was a new world, and I was worried I wouldn't know how to do anything in the new world, the world of virtual freedom.

I never believed, neither did Rashid, he said this to me, that we were ever going to get to a place past those fast visiting-room kisses. We never expected to marry while Rashid was in prison, but one lonely spring, we'd just done it. It was almost spur-of-the-moment—as much as anything can be spur-of-the-moment in a prison. *I never thought you'd marry me. Not while I was in jail, anyway,* Rashid had said, over and over. *I just didn't think you'd do it,* he'd said, amazed, grinning.

I didn't think so either, I responded. *But I couldn't wait anymore. I had to be with you.* I paused for a moment, and then I added, *I hope that you like me.*

What are you talking about, asha? I love you.

I mean sexually.

Come on, asha. Don't even go there. It would be impossible for me not to love being with you.

And I tried, I really did try to believe him. I tried not to sound defensive, but I failed, and Rashid loved to remind me so. Months later, when the sex between us had become easy, fluid, he would tease me. He'd laugh and ask me if I remembered how I was in the beginning, how I'd said,

Look. You can't touch me when I first get in there. Okay? Because I'm going to be nervous.

Okay, Rashid had said.

Look, I'm serious. Don't try to pressure me, I continued.

I won't.

I mean it, Rashid. You better relax.

No problem.

You're not listening to me. You don't understand how it is when I come in. Those police might treat me any old way. And they might make me be in any kind of mood.

What do you mean, honey?

You know how stupid these people can be, how they say dumb stuff all the time. They might put me in a bad mood. But besides that, I mean in general, I might feel nervous.

I think you said that already.

Okay. Well, I'm just trying to make sure my point gets across. You don't have to get an attitude.

First of all, I don't have an attitude, because I'm much too happy. But you know what I do think? I think you've been a pretty big talker all this time. So I guess now we see the real deal. The real deal is you want to be on some kind of virgin shit now. Think maybe you can't handle me?

Rashid could barely contain his laughter.

Fuck you, I said.

Now we talking my language! Rashid said through laughter, and then the recording came on: *You have one more minute.*

Then Rashid told me he loved me. *I love you, I love you, I love you,* he'd told me for the last time before we were together, almost like other couples: undressed, unmonitored, unrestrained, unrestricted.

venerated, sanctified

*N*ot just the first time, but whenever the date for a trailer visit comes around, everybody knows it. Friends ask if I will be free on those particular days and of course I say, *No, I'll be with Rashid.* People nod and grin and wink and then they laugh. I know that they don't mean to be insulting, but inside I twist up just a little. From my vantage point what I see is that at last here's my private moment, a moment when finally I can look at the person I love without cameras watching, and still, there's nothing private about it.

People regularly make jokes about what my time with Rashid is going to be like, until eventually I make jokes too. Nobody seems to understand that to me, the time on the trailer is sacred. It's an experience which should be spoken of in hushed and sober voices. Making love should be a holy communion.

It took me years but now I see. Before Rashid I thought making love was something my body did all by itself. My body as this independent thing, separate and distinct from my spirit, my soul. I thought making love was just this physical thing.

But the way Rashid and I would cook together, clean, tell jokes, watch television, pray, dance, stand outside in the rain, stare at each other, bathe together, massage and rock, was what I came to understand as erotica. It was what I came to understand as making love. Our sex was and is a whole thing, a circle that is everywhere present. And it is a land that, from the very first time, Rashid and I would travel to, humble, heads bowed, bearing gifts, confessions readied, and souls laid bare. And each time we have returned, we have returned in this way.

On our first trailer, Rashid picked me up and carried me over the threshold of the trailer. He carried me over to the couch and set me down easy. He did not touch me. Not immediately. He never touches me immediately, or without asking.

So I asked.

Will you kiss me?

And he did, his arms tightened around my waist, and his mouth lost itself inside my mouth. And about his hands and mouth? They were these: a river, a sail, a passport, a country, a time. A time venerated and a time sanctified. (Amen. Amen.)

night

*n*ights on the trailer are unnaturally still and silent. No loud city cars, no singing country crickets. Just a quiet immobility which belies all of those endless emotions, the love and the longing, the rage and the sadness, the desperation and the fear, the starvation and the fantasies which define and color the walls, ceilings, cells, and trailers of correctional facilities. But like everyone else who gets locked on the grounds, I have no choice. I cannot run outside and scream, cannot let my emotions overtake me. And so I do what all of us there do. I accept the unnatural, and finally, see it as normal, average, everyday bread.

The first night we lay together, Rashid and I, entangled, our breath a shared breath, I knew that never in my life had I trusted anyone as I trusted this man. Never in my life had I been naked the way I was naked with him. Naked in the way no clothes, no sheets, nor fullness of night can disguise.

With Rashid, I learned to make love the way I learned to swim. Frightened but determined, dropped into waters where the choice to survive could only be my own.

I wanted to be with Rashid in a way I hadn't ever been with a man. Before we came together, I only knew how to have sex in these two ways: as the girl who was a freak, and as the girl who was frigid. The girl who was the freak was the girl who had been trained, since she was seven years old, to act, crawl, accept, beg, dance, acquiese, stifle her screams, fake her orgasms, shake her titties, plaster a smile, and give in to every madness, at the life-threatening whims of whichever old man towered and then took over so many of her dreams. And it was always an old man. And I was always a girl.

The girl who was frigid was the girl who knew that somewhere inside herself was the capacity for great love. She was the girl who had met men who touched her at her core, but men who she feared might discover what she believed was filth beneath her flesh. She would nearly freeze when those men had touched her because she thought any honest move she made would give away the secrets that discolored her spirit.

To be in this place with Rashid, it had taken three and a half years of steady work, healing rituals, psychological research, burning candles, praying, reading astrology books, doing numerology, talking to friends in the middle of the night, and reminding myself daily that suicide was not an option. It took getting hysterical and it took Rashid accepting my hysteria and loving me back into calm. It took crying the tears my seven and ten, my thirteen and seventeen-year-old selves never could. It took going to the edge of sanity, standing on a cliff with its long drop into the jagged rocks of the crazies. It took making a last-minute parachute out of my own skin, my own bones.

But in the beginning, when I first started confronting the memories, I felt powerful seeing myself as *the victim*. After all of those years of thinking it had been my fault and my fault alone, I appreciated, even enjoyed, not shouldering the blame for the actions and illnesses of grown men.

Loving Rashid, Rashid loving me, made everything change.

I began to grow tired of not trusting or being fully happy. I began to resent the fact that, as a victim, I was expected to be weird, sad, and in need of therapy. I began to feel like I had been set up to be scarred forever, off-balance, angry, and hateful. That I was never supposed to like sex or being touched. That I was supposed to stay drunk or high or fat or addicted to nicotine. I was supposed to be everything I never wanted to be, everything I was never raised to be, and then I was supposed to die, still in pain.

But I knew that I deserved something more. I knew it wasn't fair. I conceded my childhood, my teenage years, and most of my twenties to the abuse, but I told Rashid I needed the rest of my life to belong to me. I told him this just before the first trailer visit. And that's when I knew I needed to be more than the victim I had hidden behind.

The victim was great for a time, safe for a time. She allowed me to forgive myself and allowed me to cry. The victim even gave me an identity, which was something I didn't have for those long years between seven and twenty-seven.

But ultimately, the victim couldn't save me. The victim couldn't help me create a new me, a me who trusts easily, laughs freely, and loves openly. The victim couldn't help me dance my dance, or write my poems, or enjoy my man. The victim couldn't help me tell my story, my whole story, the part of the story that does indeed smile, crack jokes, and relax at the movies. The victim couldn't help me to love kissing. The victim couldn't teach me how to share any intimate spaces. The victim couldn't summon up brand-new colors, spread them across the pages, make a brilliant new-age rainbow, toss it up into the sky, and let it spill royal purple raindrops onto my tongue.

Of course it didn't hurt, all those years when Rashid and I did not have trailers, when we were forced to actually communicate on those six-hour visiting-room dates. We were forced to become friends, best friends, before becoming lovers. Unlike all of my previous relationships, when, halfway through a discussion or disagreement, we could fall into bed, fucking our issues away, Rashid and I had no option but to talk it all through, figure out the roots of our anger and our confusion, and then to uncover our specific, individual needs. And that was how I learned what making love was really meant to be.

By the time we did finally come together, I had found the pieces of myself that had been forgotten, left in corners, swept under rugs. I told Rashid he was the first man who had all of me, the beautiful and the ugly, the perfect parts and the parts which were held together with tape and a prayer. When we entered each other, we entered and then enjoined two worlds that were previously undiscovered.

And within that moment we found home in ourselves, lush and bountiful. We found a place only we could have envisioned and crystallized, a world which pushed forward new life, pushed down old boundaries, and embraced the new moons of its own black and perfect sky.

home, revisited

*f*or hours after the first trailer, when I found myself back home, alone, I wandered in and out of the rooms in my apartment. I could not believe that Rashid was not with me. I didn't understand how, if I could feel him with me as strongly as I did, why couldn't I see him? I looked and I looked but he didn't turn up. He was not outside the door waiting for me to open up. I opened up the door anyway, checked the hallway, but did not find my husband there. I went back inside and put on an Otis Redding CD. I turned the shower on hot as I could take it, stripped, got under the water, and tried to evaporate, like the steam, like the time, but it did not happen.

For a long time after I got out of the shower, I just stood there, naked and damp. I did not pull a towel around me. I did not reach for the lotion. I did not turn away. I just stared into my reflection in the steamy bathroom mirror and began thinking about how sometimes I had felt as though I was a divorcée from my own body. It was the way I could stand back from it, study it, critique or admire it, and eventually command it. I could be so clinical that some had accused me of being unhealthy, obsessive, or simply strange. But for me, being able to stare at who I am and what I look like is progress.

For so long my body had been this hated thing, this enemy, this betrayer. I had done everything I could to ignore it out of existence. My body was Judas offering me up for shillings and rice every time I walked out the door and dared venture into a world judged by colors and shapes. By far, though, the worst betrayals came when I was fucking.

My body used to try to kill me every time I parted my lips or my legs, willingly or unwilling. It would choke me in this crazy undercover way that no one else ever noticed, but for me, there was no air. Even during the rare occasions that someone actually loved me, when my lover would take his time with me, remember the color of my eyes, even then the passageway to my lungs would sputter and finally lock itself tight into itself. My own body choked me from the inside out, letting me live only for the pleasure of its next attack. It was some wild shit.

And so that evening my eyes studying first my hard brown nipples and approving of them; my eyes moving down and accepting, if not fully satisfied with, my round though not fat stomach; and my stomach with its light-colored stretchmarks and fine line of black hair that begins at my navel and follows a straight line down to my pussy; that evening taking all of this in, taking all of this me in without cringing or critiquing, was indeed progress.

In our four years together, I had come to believe, Rashid had helped me come to believe, that even my stomach is sexy, that I am sexy. It was the way he would become transfixed on some part of me. From my eyes to my ass, he always told me, in blushing detail, how beautiful I was.

Don't no man want to feel no rock up under him, asha, he said to me during the trailer visit as we stood in front of a mirror looking at ourselves, examining who together we appeared to be.

Girl, you're the way a woman supposed to be, sweet and thick. You ain't nobody's fat so get that shit out your head. You just don't look like them sick-ass white girls from those magazines. And you not supposed to look like that. Shoot. I want a real woman. I want a Black woman. I want a fine woman. And that's what I got.

That first visit Rashid had forced me to look at myself, nude, in the mirror, with all the lights on.

Look at yourself, Momi, Rashid had said. *You so god-damn beautiful!*

I had looked because he had made me look, but I felt my pupils try to curl shut. I squinted and strained, wanting to see through myself, to see only the glass of the mirror, but it didn't work. I wanted to see my body as an indistinguishable brown mass, but Rashid refused me my selective blindness.

I watched as he smoothed his hands up my thighs, up my stomach, cupping my breasts from behind. He had run his tongue over his fingertips, and now they played with my nipples, which brought out in me an involuntary moan and then scream, arch and then grind. After all of our years of talking, all of our fantasies poured out to each other, slowly, through whispers or giggles, after all the visits when we talked because we could not touch, he knew me, and he knew that he knew me.

He knew my body, its fears, and its every nerve and yearning. He knew how my face looked when the hunger became too strong to be contained. He knew everything I had ever told him, everything I had never told him, everything I had never even thought about myself. He knew at that moment I was so desperately wet that he could have felt it down the inside of my legs if he wanted to. And he wanted to, but he waited.

He made us both wait as he smiled slightly, noticing the way my tongue and teeth played with my lips, how they reached for something to hold, to suckle, to swallow. I am telling you, I needed that man to fill me everyway and everywhere.

Have you ever loved like that, where there is no part of your lover you do not want to be touched and, finally, filled by? That's how I wanted him, in every opening I had.

Rashid kissed the back of my neck, bit the back of my neck, and whispered,

What you want, girl?

P-P-lease . . . I managed. *P-P-lease* . . . , I managed again, fearful he didn't hear me the first time.

With one hand on my back he eased me down until I was bent all the way over. My hands balanced me on the floor, his hands steadied him against my hips.

He slipped inside me naturally, with no struggle, no searching. Inside me he was tight, fitted and perfect, and I felt certain, with each sweet, long stroke he made, that I was made, like some cherished encasing, just for him.

And my lungs, they just expanded as I breathed him, as I breathed him and I breathed me, into every one of my open and wanting pores.

there are emotions
that have no name

i've never thought too often about whether or not Rashid and I should actually be allowed to have trailer visits, but every now and then there will be a talk show on and the subject will be all of the rights that people believe prisoners have. Eventually someone arrives at the issue of conjugal visits.

Can you believe it?! someone will yell. *These people go to jail and get to have sex!*

Often the people yelling are crime victims themselves who are in so much pain that the idea of anyone proposing an alternate point of view seems insane. But sometimes I imagine myself as a special guest on the show, one who cannot be interrupted.

In that scenario, I would tell them how conjugal visits are, first of all, not a right, but a privilege which can be taken away at any time. Then I would tell them that most prisoners come back out into society, and in general, the ones who do not re-offend are the ones who were able to get some schooling, learn some marketable skills, participate in alternatives to violence and in antidrug programs, and yes, the ones who were able to maintain family ties through regular and conjugal visits. I would tell them conjugal visits are not paid for with tax money, that they are paid for with various auxiliary profits associated with the prison. And I would tell them, I would stress to them, that they should not worry. Despite conjugal visits, I would say, prisons remain painfully sexually repressive environments.

I would tell them how, from the prison administration's point of view, conjugal visits lower tension; people don't want to get into trouble and lose the privilege.

I would never, ever give back the times Rashid and I have spent together on trailers. They have been among the most beautiful times in my life, filled with the most love, passion, peace, and clarity I have ever known. But there is also no question how those visits leave me, how they leave us both, awash in a loneliness and hurt as sharp and unavoidable as the rocks in the white waters of the Delaware. The hurt rushes you like that water. It yanks you unmercifully and barefoot over those rocks. It pauses for no one, and it pauses for nothing. Sometimes it feels even worse than that. It never feels any better.

Leaving Rashid. I prepare for it from the minute I arrive. By the time the clock reads 7:00 on the morning of my departure, Rashid and I are fighting. As much as we try to avoid it, some small disagreement occurs, and instead of ignoring it as I would usually do, I lose my temper. I tell Rashid that I'm glad I'm going.

I hate being here! I say to him. I scream it sometimes.

I know, baby, Rashid says. He says it every time and then picks me up, brings me over to a chair, sits me in his lap, rocks me, kisses me. *I know, baby,* Rashid says again and again and again and again. *I hate it too.* And we stay like this for the last hour before we hear the gate that surrounds the trailer site being unlocked. I start to get up. *Wait,* Rashid says. *Wait until everybody else is outside. Somebody has to be last. Might as well be us.*

Okay, baby. Okay, I whisper, and Rashid holds me tighter. *Let me kiss you one more time,* Rashid says, *while we're still alone.*

While nobody's watching. And he kisses me. He goes far, far, deep inside my mouth, and he kisses me. After this I leave. It seems unbelievable how it could happen. But it happens. I stand up. I smooth my dress. I smile. I leave.

What's it like to be separated like that? friends have asked. *It's like an enemy tank barreling over the land,* I tell them. *Except that we are the land,* I say. *We are the battleground. We are the after-effects of a scorched-earth policy.*

When a talk show or the news comes on saying how easy prisoners have it, my friends call me up. *You should write a letter,* they say. *You should tell them what it's really like,* they say, but I do not agree. There could be no one single letter to tell what it's like, all of what it's like, from top to bottom, from the inside to the outside.

There are emotions that have no name. A friend says this to me, and now I know she is right. I know it when I do sit down one day to write about what leaving the trailer feels like and find I cannot do it. I begin to imagine that I am a dancer instead. If I was a dancer, I could really explain what I felt. If I was a dancer, I think, I would use every ounce of strength I had to leap into the air, leap beyond where anyone could see, and then I would crumble down deep into the floor where I would remain while the music kept playing.

If I was the music itself, I would play in C minor, pianissimo, a concerto written for the solo cello.

And if I was not a writer and not a dancer and not a concerto, if I was still just a child, still unformed and still uninhibited, and a child who could get away with expressing whatever I wanted to, wherever I wanted to, I would just cry. I would cry from my bowels, from the deepest and most remote space inside of me, and I would never feel compelled to stop.

everywhere without

*n*ot just after a trailer visit, but on random days, it hits, the loneliness. It's like living under the constant threat of terrorism, the loneliness I live with. I never know when, like some secretly planted bomb, it will explode. Where will I be? Will I be injured? If I am injured, will the damage be permanent? Will the injuries kill me? If I am lucky enough to survive one explosion, will another come behind it and finish me off?

This is what the prison has taught me: Loneliness is a terrorist, except it has no righteous cause, no moral foundation, no God. There is no reasoning with it, none.

I can't imagine the separation, a girlfriend says to me. *What's it like, being everywhere without Rashid?* she asks.

I tell her about the first time I went to England to do a poetry reading. While I was there I stayed in Brixton, but one afternoon I was riding through central London with a friend, another poet visiting from Brooklyn. He leaned over to me, my friend did, as we rode on the top of a double-decker bus, and said as we entered Piccadilly Circus,

You know, there are no garbage cans on the street in this part of town.

Why not? I asked.

My friend looked around us, apparently checking to see if anyone could hear us, and then he whispered in my ear,

Because of bombs.

Oh, I responded. *Right, right.*

It was after this conversation that I noticed the signs posted everywhere warning people to be on the lookout for suspicious bags. Those signs, they do not let you forget that you are never really safe. Afterwards, and despite the fact that no bomb went off during my stay in England, there was this slightly edgy feeling in my stomach the whole time I was there, and every time I've gone back.

I tell my girlfriend that the streets of New York leave me with a similar uncomfortable feeling of impending disaster; not of physical bombs, C-4, dynamite, and such, but of sudden, violent, emotional eruptions. Walking in any given New York neighborhood calls up dangerous fantasies about Rashid and me being together on these streets. We are holding hands, a couple, and it is this image which is the detonator, since for me it is not the memories I have which are haunting. It's the ones which are yet to be made, the ones which I know may never be made.

New York streets and neighborhoods explode regularly in my face. They are shrapnel. They are dumdum bullets. They remind me that, too often, I do not live in the today of my life, but in a yesterday which never was, and a tomorrow which may never be.

In the streets of my New York, there are no real memories for Rashid and me. I cannot say we laughed on this block, and fought on that one, and this is why I make things up. This is why I abandon my own reality, and lose all sorts of time imagining a life that never was. We will never be teenagers together, Rashid and I. He will never save me from the isolation and self-destructiveness of my youth. I will never save him from crime and prison. But I think and think how we could have, *if only*. And I drown in that thought. I sink in it, become lost in it, lose time in it, which I cannot afford. I cannot afford to lose any more time; the prison has taken enough.

To try to defend myself against it, the loneliness, I mean, I take myself on lunch dates, dinner dates. I take myself out to the movies, and I take myself on trips abroad, on trips anywhere. But the distance between what they offer and what I need is a grand canyon. It is the real grand canyon. Whatever I lurch toward in an effort to escape the loneliness always winds up having a huge hole in the middle. It's a hole only Rashid's physical and emotional presence can fill. It's a hole so deep that if you drop anything into it, you'll never hear the landing. And it's a hole so wide that made me finally understand this thing for what it was: a worldwide organization. Loneliness. Wherever I went, whatever streets, whatever city, it had set up camp. It was always there, waiting for me.

During its reigns of terror was when I thought of her most, the widow, the murdered man's wife. What did she look like? I never knew. Rashid didn't either. The only face I knew was the one I imagined her to have. Not in the moment she learned her husband had been killed; no, that face I cannot conjure. But the one she is wearing when she turns to say something to him, Honey, would you please help me . . . , *and then it comes back, the memory, and she says, out loud to anyone and to no one,* Oh my God, he's not here. Who am I talking to?

It's that face I think I may know, not entirely, but in part. Maybe just around the eyes. I think I know it like the nightmare that repeats itself every so often: violence and separation. It's always the same frightening dream, and I cannot wake myself from it, nor predict it, nor stop it, finally. Please, can't somebody just make it stop?

two weeks later

*t*wo weeks afer the trailer visit, I began to feel sick. Everything smelled terrible and made me nauseous. No matter how much rest I got, I was tired and weak. I started watching the days on the calender. My cycle was off and I told Rashid. Two days afterwards, I told him what I had confirmed as true: I was pregnant. We were on the phone and I told Rashid just like that, with no buildup. I went right to the heart of the matter. *I am pregnant,* I said.

≈

I never thought it could happen to me. This is where I have to begin. Rashid and I didn't use protection because I never thought I could get pregnant.

I don't think I can get pregnant. I've never ever gotten pregnant, even when I was young and careless. I said this to Rashid before we had our trailer visit. I said it and I believed it with the whole of my heart. *We don't need to use any protection,* I said.

Okay, baby, Rashid said, and when the time came, he entered me and entered me, and once I even joked with him. Exhausted, I said, *Whew! Now that was some baby-making sex!* Rashid agreed and we laughed. We laughed and we did it again and again.

≈

Pregnant, I went to friends for help. I had no idea what I should do. My finances were at an all-time low, and I was on unemployment. I had just found a school willing to accept most of my credits. I matriculated and was less than a year away from finally finishing my Bachelor's degree. My days were spent going to classes, writing poetry, letters, and essays, running, and waiting for grants to come in. In no way did I feel prepared to bring a child into the world. Nevertheless, when I remember that time, I remember that I have never felt quite so necessary in the world as I did when I carried the baby Rashid and I had made.

One afternoon, a woman I am no longer friends with said, after learning I was conflicted about having the baby, that she felt powerful after she had an abortion. She told me her story in a Washington, D.C., restaurant where we were having lunch together.

You know, I was raped when I was student, she told me. *Well, the man got me pregnant and so I had an abortion. After I got rid of it, I felt so powerful, so in control of my body.*

And when she said this, I was so stunned by her comparison—me being impregnated by the man I love, her by a rapist—that I was silent. I was rigidly silent. I wanted to talk, though. I wanted to tell her that if I did have the baby I *knew* it would be a girl. *I can just feel that,* I wanted to say, but did not. I would have a summer-born girl, a Cancerian like me, a possible painter or poet, a dancer or doctor. *A baby really is like having a second chance,* I wanted to say. Me, except minus everything that ever went wrong. But I never said this to the woman that day. I never said it to anyone while I was pregnant.

Soon after the rape comment I left the restaurant, and when I did I massaged the place on my belly where I thought my baby was. I massaged it with more passion than I ever had before. That woman and I never did go back to being friends again. We spoke off and on, but after a few months had passed, we came completely apart. We did it without explanation or battle. We just came apart, but I know that the fissure began on that day in Washington, D.C.

I loved my baby. This is what I am trying to say.

There were so many obstacles. I simply could not have the baby. That was the decision I would come to and finally present to Rashid. He did not agree, however, and for the first and only time in our relationship, we became adversaries. Rashid said he felt we should go ahead. *We should have the baby,* Rashid said firmly.

We? What we are you talking about? I'm the one who's going to have to raise the baby and I'm the one who has no money, I answered.

Most Black women have no money, he argued back.

It's not the right time. I have nothing to offer a baby. Not a decent home or stable income. Nothing.

You have love. That's what children need. God knows it's what I needed when I was a child.

Look, I am not ready. Why can't you understand that? I insisted this. I insisted it as mean as I could, as mean and as adamant. But Rashid pushed through my anger. He leaned close to me, the midday sun in his eyes, sweat on his brow. His voice was low.

My mother told me once that I was supposed to be an abortion, but it was 1962 and she couldn't. She told me it had been just a year since she'd had my brother, and she and my father had split up already. She told me she was only twenty-two, and I was supposed to be an abortion. But I wasn't. By the grace of Allah. Rashid said this and then sat back. He breathed in long and deep.

And although I was shocked by this information, and although I got a fast horrible flash of what my life might have been like had Rashid never been born, I also suspected he was trying to make me feel guilty. I crunched my face at Rashid and said, *Well, she shouldn't have told you that, but it doesn't change our situation. That information doesn't make me any more pre-pared to be a mother.*

Rashid looked surprised at the lack of sympathy in my response. He implored, *asha, don't you want to have our baby?* And that infuriated me. I covered my mouth with my hands to keep from screaming *I hate you!*

Rashid, don't you want to be home to raise at least one of your babies? I countered sarcastically, and when I did, Rashid pulled back from me. His eyes turned sad, and I knew I had said the wrong thing. I knew that despite his incarceration, Rashid had done everything in his power to be a force in his child's life. He has always sent his son whatever money he could, and he has asked his family to please help, to support not just the boy, but also Dawn, the young mother who was left there at eighteen with a baby but no boyfriend.

Rashid had gone to prison one month after his boy was born. He was lucky, I told him this over and over, that his son's mother was a bright woman, a hardworking, honest woman, who never let the child be hungry, and who never interferred with Rashid having a relationship with his son.

I'm sorry, I said to Rashid. *I shouldn't have said that. About your son.*

During the time of the pregnancy, our control over our emotions spun wildly out and away from us. They spun away from me and they spun away from Rashid, and all of our visits, phone calls, and letters seemed to all spiral downward into these devastating fights. It was a horrible clash of our wills, and both of us, practiced in the art of debating, pulled out every emotional dirty trick we could to prevail over the other.

In the end, it was me. My arguments prevailed and Rashid said, *Okay, asha, you win.* I called a clinic and scheduled an appointment, and as soon as I did I knew only one thing was true: that I was a winner of nothing. I was, in fact, feeling more like I was about to lose everything.

There are things Rashid has never told me about that time. Not even now. Once when I asked him, *Who supported you when I was pregnant? Who did you talk to?* He just said quietly, *It's not the kind of thing you can talk about in prison.*

What did you feel then? I pushed.

I can't remember that time. Between the baby and our fights, it's all an ugly blur, Rashid said. *What about you?* Rashid asked me. *What did you feel? I mean besides the—you know—besides that and how bad it was, what did you feel then, asha?*

I felt guilty, I said, *and profoundly sad. And afraid. I was afraid I didn't have the thing it takes to be a good mother.*

How could you say that? Rashid exclaimed. He sat back in his chair and looked completely confused.

I hesitated and tried to figure out how to explain myself.

Just say how it was, I thought, and then began, slowly, speaking. *You know what they say about people who've been abused.* I waited for a reaction, but Rashid was just staring at me. I continued, *I was scared. I thought I might be bad for the baby. I thought I could hurt the baby.*

You would never hurt our baby, Rashid said finally. *Never.*

I know that now. But when I got pregnant, I began thinking about the abuse every day. Like when the memories first came, I explained. *It was that bad. I don't know why. When I was pregnant, the abuse informed every one of my days. Whatever else I was thinking about, I was also thinking about that. It was there, behind every story, behind every time I cried, no matter why I said I was crying. It was that, the thing. It was there.*

I wish you would have told me that. You never told me that.

I couldn't tell you. Even though I wasn't raised to believe like this, I can't help it. I have this association: motherhood and womanhood. And I was thinking about Dawn and how she brought your son up so well, and she was this standard, and she was eighteen, I was almost thirty, and even still I couldn't see doing what she had done. I couldn't see being a good single mother, raising a child you could be proud of, the way you're proud of your son. I could only see damage. I paused for moment, and then I said, *I was afraid you wouldn't want me anymore.*

That could never happen, Rashid said. *Never. I wish you would have told me all this stuff back then. We could have gotten rid of it back then.*

I wish I had told you too. But you and I both know how it was then. How we were.

Rashid nodded, and for a moment I thought I saw it again, the particular pain he wore during the time of the abortion. For a moment it seemed as though it was all there again like an avenging ghost, hovering alongside us, howling. When I saw it, I thought if only there had been some way to have known how our emotions would have run during the time of the abortion, I would have prepared myself and I would have prepared Rashid.

I could have suggested that I stay away from him, or that we limit our phone calls. I could have reread one of my books on conflict resolution. I could have found a mediator. But I didn't know better back then, and neither did Rashid, and so we fussed constantly, fought bitterly. We were no help to one another in the time of the abortion. We were only exhausted, Rashid and I. The two of us were losers. I see that now. But then I could only see and understand my own pain. Now I know that both of us had laid out our womb on a steel gurney in a mid-Manhattan clinic.

In that time, though, we would go reeling toward the very edge of the ugliest kinds of arguments, the kinds that can break a couple apart, the kinds that you cannot commit to memory, because if you did, you would just have to leave. You would have to go away forever. At least I would have had to go away. I am certain of this.

If only I had known better, though, I would have found a way to peel back all the pain, Rashid's and my own. I would have recalled the necessity of our touch. And our touch beyond the usual walls and barriers. I would have pressed us together, full and tight, flesh upon flesh, one body, one breath, synchronized and steady.

hush, little baby

*t*he night before the abortion, Rashid called to tell me he was sorry. *Baby, you know if I could be with you I would be. I'm so sorry you have to go through this,* Rashid said as his voice split in two.

Okay, I responded, disconnecting myself from myself.

Please don't be mad at me, asha.

I'm not mad.

You're something.

I'm nothing.

Don't say that, asha. Listen. I'm going to call you tomorrow. Will you talk to me? Will you tell me what happened?

Yeah.

Baby. You have to know I'm going to be there with you tomorrow.

No you won't. You're never there. You're in jail. I said this and then nothing else. We were silent for what seemed like an interminable amount of time, until Rashid took a deep breath. His voice was low, gentle.

I love you, asha. I will always love you. Always, always.

I love you more, I said, and our conversation ended there, like that, and I closed my eyes. I burrowed my head into my pillow and tried to imagine what I would feel like after my baby was gone. I tried to prepare myself.

There was no way to prepare myself. This is what I would say to Rashid when he called me after the abortion. *My sister tried to warn me,* I told him, *but I didn't listen.*

Those places are like factories, she'd said to me one morning on the phone. While I was pregnant my sister called me from her home in Los Angeles nearly every morning. *You have to be prepared for that,* she'd warned me in one of our final conversations before the procedure.

The day it happened was a Thursday and it was November and it was cold, not bitter, but unpleasant outside, very much so. I wrapped up all the way, head, neck, and hands, and took a taxi to the clinic in Manhattan. When I arrived there, I saw two people, a Black woman and a white man. They had set up a table and displayed two horrible pictures. I was sure that the pictures were of dead fetuses, but I did not look. I could not look. I stepped toward the building where the clinic is located and the couple at the table started screaming: *Don't kill your baby! PLEASE! Don't kill your baby.*

Their screams grabbed on to the hem of my coat and dragged behind me, nearly keeping me from making it through the double glass doors of the building, through the corridor and onto the elevator. I did make it, but it was a struggle. I pressed the number of the floor I'd been given, and the door closed and I began to rise. The elevator was slow. It shook. I did too. But we got there, and immediately I began to record everything, every color in that place, every scent. I knew I had to remember exactly how it was so that I could go home, write it in my journal, and later, read it to Rashid.

The elevator at the clinic opened right into a waiting room. I looked around and wondered why the the color scheme was so dark, why the decor was so synthetic. The walls were a stubborn brown, which surprised me. I did not expect something bright, no yellows or oranges, but perhaps blue, a color to soothe, to soften.

I noticed that there was nothing made of wood. There were no plants. There were only folding metal chairs, with seats cushioned in foam and black plastic. There were rows and rows of them. I started counting them. How many women can come here in a single day? Nine in the first row, seven on the side, another nine behind the seven, and then I lost track. I stopped counting and walked over to the painted gray steel counter where there were two receptionists.

Good morning, I said through a smile I had been practicing all morning.

Neither receptionist answered me. My smile faded. *I have an 8:00 appointment,* I continued.

Sign in over there, one of the women mumbled. She motioned with her eyes to a place on the counter I tried to, but could not find.

Where do you mean? I asked, still trying to be polite.

Right there, she pronounced, clearly annoyed. I signed in, and now I had an attitude as well.

For about ten minutes I sat alone in a corner of the waiting room, and then an old girlfriend of mine walked in. She took a seat next to me, hugged me, held my hand. A week before the abortion she'd called. *What's wrong?* she'd asked, *You sound terrible,* she said. I had paused for a moment and then said it, blunt, the way I'd said it to Rashid.

I'm pregnant. I'm going to get an abortion next week.

I'll be there, she'd offered with no hesitation, *since Rashid can't, I will. Don't worry.*

In all of the years that I had been with Rashid, through all of our dramas, our fights, and our marriage, I always thought I could make it alone. Prison is so isolating that you get used to handling any problems and all the pain it creates by yourself. But this abortion was Goliath, and I was no David. I could not do this alone. I accepted any love I could get. I needed every kindness I could get, every warmth. My sister and my friends, the few who knew, rose to the occasion. They called and they wrote and they listened to me. I looked at Talibah, my girl-friend from college. I held her hand tightly in mine, and then I thanked God for her. I thanked God again and again.

After thirty minutes passed, a nurse came out and called me into the back area. The woman did not say hello and she did not introduce herself. She just explained what was about to happen to me. She said,

We're doing a sonogram. Pull down your pants and underpants and lay on the table. Her voice never changed its volume or tone. I did as I was told. The unidentified woman slapped cold grease on my stomach, but she did it without saying why. For several minutes she pressed her fingers down hard onto my abdomen. It hurt and when I could not take it any longer, I said to her,

That hurts. What are we doing now?

Oh, she responded without feeling or apology. *We've got to try to get a clear picture of the size of the pregnancy so we can determine the exact age.*

You can see my—I cut myself off. What do I say now, I wondered? What noun to use? Could I still say, as I'd been saying for the last two months, my baby? Is she still my baby?

Yes. You can see it right here. She pointed to the monitor. I looked. I squinted, but I saw nothing distinguishable.

How big? I asked, meaning the pregnancy.

Well, it's hard to say . . . the nurse began.

How big? I pressed, my voice raised slightly by determination.

It's about one and a quarter millimeters, eight weeks.

And when she said this, suddenly my pregnancy became even more real to me than it had ever been before. It was, for me, the first time and only place that I had publicly been seen and confirmed as this: a woman with child. All those days on the train, walking down the street, going to school, visiting the prison, no one knew I was pregnant. There was no way for anyone to know I was pregnant, and when the pain of the situation began to march up toward me, I would trick it away. If no one around me knew what was happening to me, and if even I denied what was happening to me, was it really happening to me?

Of course that trick could not work here. Here I had no defenses. I began to cry. I cried long heaving sobs, and the nurse looked at me. Her expression did not change, but she did say, *I'm sorry.* She handed me a tissue, and then she told me we were done. She told me to go back out into the waiting room. I got up off the table, pulled my pants up, and walked back out into the room. The room with folding chairs, the brown walls, and forty or fifty women I did not know, but who would see me as many of my friends have never seen me: emotions laid completely bare, no shield, no armour.

After half an hour, a voice called me to the lab along with three other women. *It is time to take blood,* we were informed. We made fists. We stuck our arms out like some sort of strange wave. We got syringed on the assembly line. We were sent back to the waiting room.

Fifteen minutes later, someone called my name again. I was told that it was time for my counseling session, which was being handled by a woman I only ever came to know as "The

Supervisor." We sat down without greeting or introduction and began a rote process:

Social Security number? she began. I gave my number to her, and she continued, *Are you aware of other choices, adoption, foster care?*

They're not options for me, I said.

Okay, then please read and sign the release papers.

The release papers described all of the things that could possibly go wrong with the procedure. They could fail to remove the entire pregnancy, it said. I could even die. At the bottom of the page, it said that the clinic is not liable if anything happens to me. *What is your responsibility to me?* I asked. *Can I get that in writing too?*

That's not our policy, the Supervisor said. *But don't worry,* she continued almost smiling, *we've been around for years. We're licensed and regulated by the Department of Health.* Her voice glowed, and as she started telling me about the abortion itself, about what would happen when I went in for mine, I started thinking about how easy it had always been for me to be pro-choice. I started thinking about how I always believed that the idea of the government determining when a woman had to start a family was insane.

And even though I still held these beliefs as I sat there in that counseling session, something visceral, something at the very core of me, felt shaken, out of place, wrong, when it was me about to have *one and one quarter millimeters* of my womb scraped out and left in a hazardous waste material bag. It was going to be scraped out and I was going to call it freedom but I didn't feel free and I didn't feel good. I felt confused and terrified and I wondered if she could understand that. I wondered if she knew she was looking at a mother in mourning. Her voice pinched on in the background of my thoughts. I faded in and out of what she was saying: . . . *A hundred women we service every day* . . . , and, *over before you know it* . . . My teeth began to grind, my fists tightened. Eventually I signed the papers and got sent to another reception area, one closer to the operation room.

Only one other woman was there waiting alongside me. She was tiny, except for her belly. Later I learned she was five and a half months pregnant. Later I learned she was getting an abortion too, but while mine took between five and fifteen minutes, hers took place over a three-day period. I tried not to stare at her swelling. I thought about how babies were often born prematurely, my God, at six months. In only two months from then, a girlfriend of mine would in fact give birth to her baby, a beautiful girl, who was born after only a five-month pregnancy.

But I pushed my negative thoughts away. I did not want to judge the woman sitting next me. I did not know the specifics of her story, why she was there on that Thursday in November. What I did know was that she was in a lot of pain. Water was squeezing out from every part of her. Her breath was chopped into tiny pieces. She begged for painkillers and a nurse with a voice as rough and hard as a prizefighter's hands said,

Honey, I just gave you one. You're fine! And then she disappeared through a door. I moved next to the small woman with the big stomach. I took her hand in mine. I took it as gently as I could. *Come on,* I whispered, *I'll do deep breathing with you. It'll help. Inhale as deep as you can,* I said, *Like this,* and I breathed through my nose, sucked the air down to my diaphragm, and exhaled through my mouth. I did it the way I had learned to do in yoga class. The woman tried her best and together we breathed and together we prayed. *Please, God, let the pain go away. Or at least go down. Please, God, please.* It was me who said this. *Amen,* the woman whispered. *Amen,* she whispered again, and we continued holding hands, but we said nothing else. Not even when the nurse came to get me. We did not even say good-bye when I rose to leave. We said nothing at all. We did not need to.

The nurse took me up in an elevator, up into a room where another woman, not a nurse, told me to *Strip all the way down, honey, like you takin' a shower.* I stripped and put on the hospital robe they provided me with. An air conditioner blew cold air on my back, but I did not feel cold. I did not feel anything. Another nurse appeared in another doorway and told me to follow her. She brought me into a tiny room with big bright lights and a steel gurney in it. In the corner of the room was the hazardous waste material bag, my baby's humble coffin. It was red, the bag, and I stared at it as another nurse walked in and began to rattle off instructions:

Sit down on the table, slide down to the end, lie back.

I did as she asked while tears and hysteria began to redefine my face. I did not even try to calm down. The anesthetician came in. He was cheerful and bouncy. He said,

Hi, honey. I need your arm. But listen, you've got to stop crying. It'll impair your breathing. Okay? Can you go ahead and do that for me?

Then the nurse said softly, *Don't be scared, you're going to be fine. It'll be over before you know it.*

The doctor entered and introduced himself. In the four

hours I spent in that clinic, that was the first and only time I learned someone's name. I tried to introduce myself as well, but the crying slashed my words. It ripped them down incomprehensibly. I babbled and the doctor continued,

Hey, what you crying for? I haven't even touched you yet.

My legs were strapped into stirrups. *That was the last thing I remember,* I said to Rashid a day and a half later, *before waking up in the recovery area.* I told him that when I woke, I tried to sit up immediately, but still slightly dressed, fell back. I could not run out, but I wanted to. I just lay there. I looked around me. I was surrounded by women, perhaps twenty of them. They were in hospital beds like mine, in robes like mine. I thought that yesterday we all were pregnant, today not one of us is. Today, not a single baby among us. A recovery room nurse came over to me. *Hello,* she said, in a voice so kind I thought my heart would shatter.

Please don't leave me, I whispered, I begged. *I don't want to be alone. Please,* I said again and again, *Please.*

I told Rashid how the nurse was nice, how she was the first really nice person I'd met at the clinic, and I told him how I was crying but no water was coming out of my eyes and how this made me panic, how I thought maybe my whole body had become dysfunctional, useless, worn-out, upside-down, wrong-side-out. *That's not true, that's not true,* Rashid said when I told him these things. *We will have beautiful babies one day, asha. This was the wrong time. But you are the right woman. To be with me, to have my babies. You always have been the right woman. You always will be the right woman,* Rashid said.

After he said this I was quiet for a moment, and then, out of meanness and pain, *Still feel like you were there with me? In spirit and all?*

Please don't do that, asha, Rashid said. *I can't fight with you. I just cannot do it. Anyway, the important thing is whether or not you felt like I was there.*

And although I was hurting and angry and empty, my womb was empty anyway, I refused to lie to Rashid. I would not withhold the truth from him. *Yes,* I whispered, *I did, baby. I really felt like you were there,* I said. I paused for a few seconds and then said, *Rashid?*

Yes, baby?

Did I tell you that I felt hated in that place? Did I tell you I didn't understand how I could have felt so hated there?

It's a clinic, baby. People get under pressure and forget how to act. But they didn't hate you. asha? Rashid asked.

Yes?

Do you know I love you, girl? I love you so much. You have to know I love you so much. We're going to get past this. I promise you that. And then the computerized operator came on. *You have one more minute,* it says, and we say good-bye. We got off the phone and I crawled into bed. I pulled the covers around me, put my hand between my legs and held it there. I held it like I was trying to keep anything else from falling out of me. Falling out or being pulled or cut or scraped out. *Good night,* I said out loud from under my covers. *Good night, my baby.*

And my eyes searched the room for some sign from the baby who will never be mine. I wanted a breeze to push through the room. I wanted my candle to flicker out and then back on again. I wanted the branch on the tree outside my window to move. I wanted something to fall off the wall, a lightbulb to go out, but none of this happened.

My room was entirely still. The baby that could have been, but never would be mine, was gone. And that's all there was.

Nothing else. No more to say or think or hope for or imagine. She was just gone, my baby. I repeated that just under my breath. *She's gone,* I said aloud so I could make myself believe it. I chanted it and I chanted it. The last two months were real. There could be no denial. They did happen, and the baby did happen, and the baby did not happen. I chanted so I would remember everything. I chanted so I would never ever return to this place. *She's gone, she's gone,* I said and I said. And then finally I became still, and I became quiet. For the next few hours I lay in bed and I did not speak, and I did not sleep, and I did not move.

after

almost three weeks after the abortion, I was sitting one morning in the visiting room sipping on bad vending-machine coffee. Inside, I felt something which had been foreign to me for so long. I felt at peace. I felt easy with myself. *This is it,* I thought, *my life,* with all its burdens, but also with all of its blessings.

I began to see those blessings again, all the love in my life, the creativity, the hopes and possibilities, the friends and the family. I saw the blessings and they were the lighted roads I had been seeking. The ones which send me, protected, over and over, out into the world. The ones which bring me back home again.

On that morning of peace in the visiting room, Rashid asked me to put the coffee aside, and I did. As he often does when he is about to be serious with me, he took my face in his hands. We were so close that I could not see him, but I felt him, breath, skin, sweat, and pulse.

Welcome back, he said to me.

Excuse me?

You haven't been yourself since this whole thing, but I noticed the last two times on the phone and this morning even, you're back to being my asha. Smiling asha. Silly asha. Laughing and sweet asha. It was really lonely without you here. So, welcome back.

I put my arms around Rashid, and I draped both of my legs over his legs. I checked to see if the police noticed how we were sitting—me practically in my husband's lap, straddling

187

him. We were lucky. If the police did notice us, for some reason they did not come over and repeat the rules:

Excuse me, Mr. Rashid, please tell your wife to keep her feet flat on the floor and her chair and her person on her side of the table at all times.

Uninterrupted by rules, I continued, *I never even considered having any man's baby until you,* I whispered. *But this wasn't the right time, was it, honey?*

Rashid shook his head slowly, and then looked at me. He said nothing. He just held me. He held our emotions, our hurt, and all of our hope in his arms. He held me and it was a brilliant morning. Even the visiting room with its shaded windows and lifeless colors could not mask it. It was a brilliant morning and my beloved was holding me. He was holding me so thoroughly that I could tell him anything, deny him nothing, give him everything.

Whenever I have thought I could not love Rashid more, and whenever I have thought I could not be more naked with him, he will say something to me, or he will do something for me, or else he will just touch me in this way that makes me want to find a part of myself that I have somehow forgotten about and turn it over to him.

This was what I was thinking that morning and I began to fidget slightly in Rashid's arms. He asked me what was wrong. *Aren't you comfortable?* he asked me.

Yes, I said. *Of course,* I said. *It's just that I want to tell you something.*

What is it, baby?

I turned to face Rashid and kiss him. *Come here,* I said, *so I can whisper to you.* He leaned toward my mouth. I kissed his ear and then said softly, *I can't wait to one day have your baby. If I ever get pregnant again, even if it's before you come home, I'm going to have your baby.*

And when I said this, Rashid held me tighter and the police did not bother us and the sun pushed through the thick glass and shades and rested on our backs and we were still, my beloved and I. We were completely at peace, and we remained that way, still and at peace, calm and resolved, without words, and without movement, and without tears, for a very, very, very long time.

no strings attached

We were in the dead of winter, a winter with neither relief nor pause, except that at last we had been given our second trailer. I was a little scared. I wanted to make love with Rashid, but sex was no longer this thing to simply fantasize about and enjoy. Sex was this thing which could produce life. I went to see my husband armed with a diaphragm, spermicide, warnings, and condoms.

After waiting to be processed for three hours in the room that had no chairs, no water fountain, no vending machines, nothing, we were walked into the facility. The site holds four trailers, and as soon as the guard unlocked the gate, our husbands and sons came rushing out to us. Rashid always leads the group and always greets me with a big smile and a bigger hug.

Let me take that for you, baby, he said on the afternoon that our second trailer visit began. He took my garment bag off of my shoulder. With his other hand he lead me over to our trailer. When we got to the door he said, *Wait a second, honey.*

Rashid placed the bag down, just inside the trailer. As he had done on the first visit, he picked me up and carried me over to the couch. He sat beside me. We held each other, in a sense no differently than when we are in the visiting room, but somehow it was completely different. Boundaries were gone, well, temporarily set aside.

Can I kiss you? Rashid asked, moving, kneeling over me.

Yes, I said, and arched my body upward to receive him.

Rashid eased into our kiss, memorizing first my lips, and

then my tongue, and then behind my teeth. He kissed me as though I could disappear if he did it wrong. He kissed me as though I could break. He kissed me as though he could break.

I pulled Rashid on top me, deep into my breast. Beard, tears, and flesh, we were all one entity seeking air, comfort, life-affirming touch. *Has anyone else ever seen you like this?* I wondered, holding him tight as my arms would allow.

I looked at Rashid, past his skin, pores, sinew and lines. I peeled away his thirty-four years until once again he was tiny, a boy of only nine, maybe even seven. *Did anyone love you then as a child is supposed to be loved, unconditionally, thoroughly, no strings attached?* I thought this, but I did not say it. *Do I love you like that now?*

What I knew was that I loved my husband as best as I possibly could. But within the bizarre reality of our monitored life, would my best ever be good enough to erase this stark landscape or his demons? Would my best be good enough to cleanse his open sores and help him create wholeness out of the charred and scattered pieces of himself? What *has* Rashid lost along his own particular trail of tears, from Guyana to the South Bronx, from the South Bronx to Rikers, from Rikers to almost every maximum-security correctional facility in New York State? Small remains of who he is and was and hopes to be: How were we to gather them all up, keep what's necessary, discard what's not?

Momi, Rashid said to me bravely, *I just don't know that it's fair to you, I mean, keeping you here. I feel selfish. You could own the world, and look. You're here in a trailer on a prison ground. I feel like I hold you back, but I need you, Momi. Please never hate me. I love you so much.*

My tongue played over the light tears on his face. I caressed

Rashid with my lips. I felt it was the best response I could give at the moment. Had I actually spoken, what would I have said? My head was telling me he was selfish. That he should let go. That he never should have brought me here. He should have been a dog, uncommunicative, irresponsible, abusive, *a typical man*. A man I couldn't love.

But my body, heart, and spirit stood in defiant and diametric opposition to my head. I felt more than love for Rashid. I believed in, respected, and *enjoyed* getting lost in him. Over the years, his love had been enough to make me withstand being a woman who went home every night of every day to dinner for one and an empty bed. The fullness of his love allowed phone-call fantasies to replace an evening on the town.

I let the warmth and wet of my body disguise my ambivalence and fears and all of my hurtings. *Make love to me, Momi,* Rashid pleaded, hushed and hungry. I did not hesistate. We have these forty-four hours together every three to five months. I knew and he knew there was not a second to spare. I knew and he knew exactly what we have always searched for. We knew where it was. We knew how to get there.

I removed what little clothing Rashid still had on and asked him to step back, to let me look at him. It had been over three months since the first and only time that I saw my husband naked. I stared at the faint scar on his abdomen. I touched it. My fingers tried to recall a memory my eyes could not. Had this scar been here before? It had to have been. It was an old mark. It looked like a childhood mark, faded and comfortable in its place. I stared and stared but the memory did not come. Right then, had I made the attempt, I could have convinced myself that this was the first time that I ever saw my husband nude.

My arms circled Rashid around his hips. My mouth moved toward his close, closer. I began to taste him down his stomach, down the inside of each thigh. I swallowed part and then all of him, until he screamed, moaned, arched, begged me to ride him. I moved him down to the couch and slipped on top of him. My hands were flat, spread across his chest. The ride began. Slowly at first. We didn't want to rush. We wanted to keep things as they were, in perfect balance.

I tilted my head toward the ceiling and just above my head I saw our dreams beginning to paint the air. Our bodies coasted. They became a multicolored magic carpet. They were a deep purple uptown Cadillac, a black horse with wings that could fly us out of this madness.

Rashid pulled me until I was down on his face. My nose to his nose. My lips against his lips. And my nipples against his nipples. Our sweat was the holy water our throats had craved forever. *Don't move, baby . . . let me hold you,* Rashid said, pressing his hands into the small of my back. *Let me do this, Momi,* he continued, pumping upward and into me.

This is what they say, baby . . . in those books . . . to feel like you're one person with your lover . . . I . . . feel like we're one, Rashid panted. And we were. We were in tune, intuitive, indefatigable, inexorable.

And then the phone rang. Right there, right then, unbelievably, the phone rang. It was a guard. It could only be a guard. The phones on trailers are one-way phones. They allow police to call and check on us whenever necessary. Rashid slid out from beneath me, picked up the receiver, and a voice was so loud that even I, several feet away, could hear it. It was time for the count.

Rashid pulled on his state green pants, black boots, and

white sweatshirt. He inhaled deeply, opened the door, and stepped outside. He stood there waiting for the guard to come around and verify his presence. This check happens seven or eight times during every visit.

After it was determined that Rashid and the three other men who were having a trailer visit were exactly where they were supposed to be, the guard yelled into a walkie-talkie that the count was clear. My husband came back inside.

Back inside he found me where he left me, only now I was wrapped up tight inside the blankets and sheets we had previously discarded. When Rashid had opened that door, when he had stepped outside, I'd become desperately cold. Desperately cold and suddenly alone, I had pulled the blankets around me and watched him as he had gone through the door.

Rashid has said that when we are old, we will remember little of this time. *No room for bad memories, because we're going to crowd our lives with good ones.* My husband is an optimistic man. He always has been. For as long as I've known him. But I know that when I am old and these years are a long time past us, despite any good memories we may one day create, what I will always remember about the prison experience is how it was being on trailers. The two of us there, always together, always alone.

the prisoner's wife

*h*ave I said how almost every prisoner I have ever known has told me when I asked that he's coming home in just one minute? *One minute.* Not ten minutes, not fifteen, but one minute. Even the brothers I've met who are doing thirty years with life on the back. *When you coming home, Pa?* I'll ask. *I'll be home in a minute, girl,* he'll say to me, and mean it. And I would look into his face wet with sincerity, and think, okay, sure. Whatever you say. And as though the brother could read my doubts, he would inevitably and with considerable passion add, *You'll see, girl. I'm going to be home in one minute. Yeah. In one minute.*

Have I said that Rashid told me that he would be home in one minute as well? He said it like this, over and over: *Mama,* he would begin, *Mama, I got this. I'm telling you, baby. I'm going to get some rhythm with the feds. I knew in the state courts my issues weren't as clear. I never really expected to win an appeal in the state. But I had to go through them to get to the feds. Remember? I explained all that to you. Remember? I told you when you first got with me.*

I remember, baby.

But the feds are different, asha. I know I got the law on my side with them.

Really, baby?

I'm telling you, girl. I got this.

Have I said that I've worked around legislators in my life, that I have some idea about how they think, what influences how they vote? And have I said that I listen to people, average, everyday people, in hair salons and on airplanes, when I go to get my nails done, when I go to the gym? I hear the rage and the unwillingness to talk, to discuss crime and criminals, transformation and mercy. When Rashid talked about his appeal, I talked about the social and political climate in which he was making that appeal. *That ain't got nothing to do with the law,* Rashid said.

What does, then? I asked.

Look, the law is the law, baby. It's already on the books and it's on my side. Rashid said this, with his back straight, his smile wide.

Have I said how Rashid can argue the law, argue it like a seasoned attorney, perhaps even better, because it's his own life he's fighting for? And how Rashid can write a brief that you would never guess wasn't written by a lawyer, which is why I couldn't fight him when he said he was going to win the appeal. The law was his territory, Rashid used to say that. He would say it and then back it up by quoting cases and precedents.

Writing's your territory, Rashid has said to me, *but the law is mine. I wouldn't question you if you told me that a letter or article I wrote was all messed up, and I think you should trust me when I tell you things about the law. I wouldn't tell you law I wasn't certain about. You have to have some faith in what I know, baby. You have to have some faith in me.*

Okay, I said. I said it because I did have faith in him. Because I would never have been in that prison for a single second if I didn't have faith in my husband, a big, ever-growing faith. And this is why I resigned. I took Rashid's hand in my hand. I looked at him directly, and I said, *You're right. You're right. I believe you, honey.* I gave in to his arguments, each one of them. Have I said that? How I gave in of my own free will? I gave in and all the while knew I was ignoring the voice inside myself that warned me to keep my defenses up. The voice that admonished me to balance faith with reality. But I ignored it at every turn. I just listened to my husband and became a believer. I believed because I wanted to believe. I wanted to believe whatever he said about the law and his case and the appeal and how he would get a time cut and how he would be home in the next two years and how no matter what, there was just no way the state was going to keep him for all that time. I believed this. I did. I did.

Have I said how often somebody will look at me, flush with concern, place their hand on my shoulder, wrinkle their brow, and ask in a whisper, *So, asha, when is Rashid coming home, anyway? How much longer do you all have to go?*

A minute, I say to them. *Rashid will be home in just a minute,* I repeat, and then I disappear inside myself. I disappear inside my prayers. I concentrate. I meditate. I summon up faith enough for a hundred women, maybe even more, and I begin to pray. But I do not pray to just any God. I pray to every God I have ever heard of. I call out whatever name, in whatever manner of worship. I am loud and I speak in tongues. I am soft and I whisper just below my breath. I sob and then I am stoic. But no matter how I go to meet God, two things never change. Every time I go, I go begging and I go ready to deal.

Sweet Jesus (Mary? Joseph? Peter or Paul?), Allah, Jah, Yemaja, Ra, Obatala. Buddha, Kali Ma, Oh Great Spirit, You, You whose name cannot be known or spoken. Look, look. Can you see me, arms out, reaching into the four winds? Jesus, here I am, here, here, genuflecting at the altar, swallowing bread and wine. Allah, I'm facing the Ka'ba on my knees. My forehead is to the ground. Can you see me, Obatala, Yemaja, Ellegba? I'm here at the crossroads stand-

*ing in need of direction, a signpost, a tiny clue, a piece torn from a
map. Where am I? Am I as lost as I think I am? Am I close, am I
far? Am I hot, am I cold? Can you see me, who can see me? Can you
hear me, who can hear me? Who's willing to come bargain with the
prisoner's wife?*

*Listen. I have already given up cigarettes and wine, and after
today I will stop cursing. I'll leave short tight dresses in the back of
my closet. I'll cover my hair. I'll stop eating sugar. I'll stop drinking
coffee. Is there more, do you want more? That's no problem. I'll drop
my fast, mean judging of people. I'll be more patient. I will never tell
another lie. I'll never stretch the truth again. I will grow more love
in my heart. Can You see me trying, Lord? You have to see how hard
I am trying. Were you there when I went to the park at six o'clock
that Sunday morning surrounded by six of the people closest to me?
We washed our hands, feet, and faces. We lit black and red candles
in the wind. We stood in the presence of You and of our ancestors. We
synchronized our prayers, and the six of us called on You. Did You
hear us? Our voices rising into one voice. Can You just tell me if You
heard us? If You or even one of Your angels heard us that morning,
or later when I was home alone, praying out loud, trying to lean
against my own shadows, imploring them for support. They did not
support me, my shadows. They were too busy dancing. Did You see
that, how my shadows abandoned me to go dance on the wall? They
danced on the wall where Rashid's picture is hanging. I was jealous
of how my own shadows could dance with Rashid. I wanted to dance
with him. I wanted to dance for him and I said so that night. I said
it out loud. I want to dance with and for my husband. Did You hear
me when I said it? Did anyone hear me? Anyone at all? Anyone?
Anyone?*

Have I said what it sounds like when a heart breaks inside a
prison? It doesn't sound like a crash, and it doesn't sound like a

shatter. When a heart breaks inside a prison, if it sounds like anything at all, then it sounds like a scream that's trapped in a building caught on fire. It sounds like a scream that is not female and that is not male. It is just human, the scream, human and desperate, and it tries to throw itself high, up and over the hysterical pitch of the sirens, and the greedy chomping of the flames. It tries but it does not succeed.

It does not succeed and finally, exhausted, it falls back where it gets vanished into a bigger, meaner orchestra of screams that comes from the fire and that comes from the sirens. The little human scream gets surrounded, enveloped, and then neutralized. My scream, or her scream, or her scream, or his, are turned, without mercy, into ashes and soot. They are turned into ashes and soot and are then left behind to be rinsed or washed away forever.

Have I said that prison is a fire that seems to always be able to roar the loudest, to spread the furtherest, to swallow the most, and to spare the least?

slipping

We lose the appeal. It is July, the month of my birth, and Rashid tells me the news one hot afternoon when I am visiting him. We are standing outside. Not outside exactly, but in a cage that is attached to the visiting room. The ceiling of the cage is nearly open, but the air is blocked by the crisscrossing razor wire. Still it is better somehow than being indoors, we pretend it is, and in fact, a tiny wind hangs between us and cools itself along our foreheads.

Rashid tells me that we have lost, and I nod my head. *Yes, yes,* I say, although I do not know why. I am certainly not affirming the decision, but perhaps it is a response to the question Rashid does not ask me, the one that I know is lurking behind the bad news: *(You going to stay with me, baby)?*

Yes. Yes, I say it again and then fade for a moment into the pain, the loss, the reality of it. *Okay,* I say, and pull my husband toward me. I try to comfort him. I hug him, but not very hard because I do not have the strength to hug him very hard. My strength lies between us on the floor. I see it there, splattered and useless.

My arms are closed weakly around Rashid's waist. I nod my head again. Nod because I keep hearing the bad news in my head. I hear it in stereo. I hear it like a gun being fired just past my ear. *We lost the appeal! We LOST the appeal!! WE LOST, WE LOST, WE LOST, WE LOST!!* The words are an automatic loaded with dumdum bullets, an Uzi hung out a car window, spitting death into the tree-lined street.

And for two months afterward, I will negotiate my days as

though I am in mourning. I am functional in life, but not passionate about it. The only time I allow any emotion to roam freely is when I am with Rashid. When I am with him, I allow his needs, his desire, his unbelievable optimism to fill the gutted rooms inside me. With Rashid, I laugh, I tease. With Rashid I am sexy and warm and driven by his faith. With Rashid I can lay visions onto the concrete walls around us and over and over I can say, *Yes, yes. (I'm going to stay with you, baby.)*

And then something starts to shift, not shift so much as fall flat, as flat as the words which begin to fill the journal I write in each morning, dull, starched, ironed-down, burned, unusable words. No matter how hard I try, and I do, I try for weeks and weeks, I lose the language, and then the desire to pretty the situation up. Even with Rashid, I am limp. All I can think about is what decor can I hang upon another seven years locked down, away? What ornaments, what trinkets, what bright lights, what color paint? And when I begin to ask these questions, there is nothing Rashid can say, no comfort he can offer, no possible solution, no new vision that can snatch me back into dreaming with him. I become consumed with anger.

I go back and back and back and back. What did Rashid say and when did he say it? What arguments had he erected, what promises had he made? In a fit of hysteria one night, I storm through my apartment and pull boxes of his letters out of the closets. I scour them for the hope Rashid sent me again and again and again. I read letters that cited cases, letters that talked about time cuts. Letters that said, *When I come home, which will be sooner than you think . . .*

I sit for hours one evening in the middle of my room surrounded by hundreds of letters. I think if I can gather them up, show Rashid where he promised me, maybe things will be all right again. Maybe he will fix it so we do win the appeal. For the whole of our relationship, Rashid has always been an honest man. If only I can confront him with his own words I know he will turn things around. Rashid, the strong. Rashid, the honest. Rashid, the beautiful. He cannot, fast as night, become Rashid, the liar. Rashid, the terrible. Rashid, the enemy.

Of course this does not happen. I confront Rashid and he can only apologize, can only say,

Baby, I told you what I believed was true.

But his sincere beliefs are not good enough for me. I return to my anger and I return to it silently, without warning. I just go back, and eventually Rashid notices, but I admit nothing, deny everything. Rashid pushes. He interrogates me about the way I have suddenly become too tired to hold up my end of the conversation, and what about how I have become too busy to come and have a visit with him? Rashid asks me these questions again and again, but I am resilient. Even the way I say hello, Rashid declares one day, even then, I sound different. I listen but only say,

Really?

What's wrong, baby? You have to tell me. Don't keep your feelings all to yourself.

Yet this is exactly what I want to do. My feelings are all I have, all that I can keep and control, all that won't change unless *I* so determine it. Besides this, I know he will only tell me the two things I want least to hear. He will tell me things are going to be all right, but he will not say how, and he will not say when. After, he will tell me I knew what I was getting into when I fell in love with him. He will say this confidently as though there was some manual in existence, some workbook. And he will say this as though on that first visit or second, he had warned me, *Listen, asha, there will be many nights when you will be lonely, and frustrated, and feel defeated.*

We live with this, my tight silence, for weeks. It seems that in those weeks we relive every long year already gone to the prison.

Yet, there are moments when I lurch toward disclosure, toward explaining how I feel and why. During phone conversations, there are a number of times when Rashid's insistent warmth and love overwhelm me. And I know if we were together, I would yield beneath his touch, beneath the very hint of it, but we are apart. We are apart and I am not visiting him very much, and this forces us to grasp at one another across telephone wires. With that barrier in place, the need to protect myself proves greater. It snatches me back one time, two times, three times, four.

And then one night I have a dream. I'm not usually the one who remembers dreams, that's Rashid's specialty, but this one is so clear that I wake up with a new vision. I pick up my journal and in it I begin to write my husband a letter.

I feel myself slipping. This is how I begin the letter to Rashid, the letter in the journal. The letter about my dream.

I am slipping, I write, *but not in the way you would think, as though the ground has suddenly turned slick, like black ice in winter. But slipping as if I have been dropped down a great, deep well. This was the dream, but the dream is alive, the dream is my life.* I say this in the letter.

I am in the well and I am screaming to get out, screaming but nobody can hear me, and finally my voice fails.

My hands, then, I think, and I pound and I pound with them against the stone walls of my cage, and at last I am heard. It is you (Rashid) and you turn your arms into a thick, rough rope. You lower the rope that is your arm and I reach it, but only when I stand on the very tips of my toes. I grab on but the rope burns, and this is when the slipping begins again, slipping now from the burning, slipping from the fire. The rope that is your arm is cutting into me, and it is going one way, and I am going the other way. You know it, I know it.

Come on, you say to me, *comeon comeon comeon.*

I'm trying, I yell up to you, *but my hands are burning.*

Stay with me, asha, you plead. *Stay with me, baby. You can do this. We can do this. Come on. Comeoncomeoncomeon.*

In my dream Rashid's voice is a drum, although not a beat above me, and not a beat beside me. It is a beat inside me, his voice, inside me like the music of my childhood used to be inside me, the music of my teenage dancing years, the music which had been the one consistent joy during those years.

Back then, songs organized all of my movements. They determined who I was friends with, what I did on weekends, everything. But as I grew older, I tried to gain control over my life, and I stopped drinking and hanging out and going to clubs, and fusing all those Friday nights into Saturdays on flashing, heated, dance floors. And when I let all of it go, I let the music go too. I did not understand how the song and the beat were not the problem.

But it forgave me, my lost music did, and now it had returned to me. I could hear it and I could also see it. My music had returned in a dream, not with the lights, and not the crowds, but the beat inside was back again in the voice of my beloved. It carries me, that voice, that drum, and suddenly I become weightless. Suddenly my hands do not burn. In the dream, I begin to feel myself being lifted out of the well.

How did you do it? I want to know this from Rashid as soon as my body edges up over the top of the dream-well. *How, how?* Rashid's arms are around me. He is sitting, I crawl into his lap.

I don't know what I did, he says. *I don't know.*

I want Rashid to tell me something! To explain how he got me from down there, to back on top, and the whole time, no magic, no rescue squad, no fancy technology. I question and I question, but finally, there is only us, Rashid and me, there, alone, and the dream ends. I wake up and make myself a cup of coffee and pull out my journal and begin to write:

The pain of our separation is a vise and we pull on it, and we pull on it, until it gives. It opens up, that vise, never completely, but enough so that we are able to move. We are able to declare that it has lost in the end, to you, and to me, and to the people we are, and to the people we are trying to become.

a difficult monologue

*t*here came a Saturday morning, late in the autumn after Rashid lost the appeal, when I was on my way upstate to the prison. Everything seemed the same. The van pulled into the South Bronx to pick up the last few passengers, and I got out of the van to go get a cup of coffee, but the usual sense of excitement I felt because I was about to see my husband had been replaced by exhaustion and frustration. I felt especially crowded and discomforted by the normal early Saturday city noises and movements: the car radios pumping Biggie and R. Kelly, the school-age children and their frantic mothers crying and whining, and all the fly girls who had just left the after-hours spot chattering over the barking and bravado of the men who flank them.

It was not yet seven o'clock, yet all this life was walking and rushing beside and then past me. It astonished me. It nearly staggered me, and then it stilled me. I watched and watched and the more I watched, the more I became immersed in a sense of isolation. Where did I fit in, here in the messy, loose, late-night, early-morning, smeared-makeup, cacophonous world? And as I was wondering this and feeling sorry for myself, Freddie the van driver came over. He told me to get on the van, which was really not a van. He was using a minibus to accommodate an increased number of passengers. Freddie laughed and said, *Come on, asha. Aren't you ready to see your husband?*

Yes, I nodded and dragged myself and all of my emotions onto the minibus where I found that the double seat which I had occupied alone before I went outside now contained a pretty young woman.

Excuse me, I said to her and slid into my seat. *Good morning,* I said to her and hoped she was pleasant.

Good morning! she chirped, which made me notice her for real, because it is a rare thing to meet someone on the way to a prison who chirps at you.

I smiled at the young woman and thought she could not be any older than twenty-one. Later I would find out that I was right. I would find out that this young woman who was talkative and bright was nineteen years old. I would find out that she was Dominican, that her name was Elisabeth, and that her man was doing twenty-five to life on a felony murder conviction. She would tell me these things without my prompting. She would tell me because she needed to talk as much as I needed to connect with someone. There was no one in her family, the young woman would explain to me, to whom she could really talk. They didn't understand why she stayed with Tony, her boyfriend, after he was convicted, and her friends didn't really understand either, she would tell me.

I understand, I said.

The nineteen-year-old woman beside me named Elisabeth was pretty, with wide, bright brown eyes, long, curly hair that she had not tried to manage, and red, red lips. She told me she met Tony while they were in high school and that she had always loved him. *From the beginning,* she told me. *I loved him right away and I've never stopped,* she told me.

I understand that too, I said.

Elisabeth told me about the crime, a story about a robbery gone bad and how no one was supposed to die, but the cashier who also turned out to be the owner reached for his own pis-

tol, and out of fear and nervousness, Tony squeezed the trig-
ger. *Just once,* the young woman said, as though this was a jus-
tification. *He never meant to kill nobody. His best friend was in the
car waiting, and at the trial that's who testified against my
boyfriend, and all the lawyer could do was say sorry, but you know,
he still took the last installment check. Even though nothing he
promised came true, that man just took the money and Tony's
mother is not a rich woman. She had pulled together every piece of
money she ever had. She borrowed money and she sold stuff to save
her son because the lawyer had promised her. He looked her dead up
in the eye and said the only evidence was the best friend's testimony
but he could get that knocked out. But he was wrong. My man got
twenty-five to life. Did I tell you that? Twenty-five to life!*

Yes, I said. *You told me.*

*Tony already did two years on Rikers. That's where he's coming
from now. This is my first time upstate,* she said, and then paused
and then added, *You know, he was a good student in school. Not as
good as me, but he got mostly B's. Sometimes C's. But mostly B's. I
got mostly A's.*

Elisabeth would tell me again how people in her family
wanted her to get on with her life and how sometimes, just
sometimes, even she thought she should get on with her life, but,
she told me, she had no idea how to leave, loving him the way
she did. *I know,* I said. *I really, really know that feeling,* I empha-
sized. And then Elisabeth concluded her story. She said, *Anyway.
I know he's coming on home kind of soon because of the appeal.*

The appeal? I asked.

Yeah, she said. *Everybody knows for sure that he got an unfair
trial,* she said, as I looked at her, trying not to betray my feelings, trying to keep my gaze steady, my face from twisting up.

I turned my body away from hers as naturally as I could. I

sat straight back in my seat. I closed my eyes and did not tell her that everybody did not know for sure that he got an unfair trial. I did not tell her that even if they did know for sure, it still might not make a difference, and I did not tell her what I did know for sure.

I did not say that she, *for sure,* should not count on her man coming home on appeal. That, *for sure,* the chances of that happening were very, very slim. At best. I did not say that if she stayed, she was, *for sure,* in for a terrifically long, lonely ride, the kind of ride that makes you begin talking to yourself, and that whatever she was predicting for her tomorrows ought to be turned loose right now. I did not tell her how six years ago I believed in things that today I cannot even comprehend. I just listened to this young woman because maybe. Maybe things would be different for her. Maybe she would never look up, as I have looked up, and realize how much prisons defined her life. Maybe she would never come back from a correctional facility as I have come back from a correctional facility, and stood there motionless in front of my own door for many, many seconds, nearly a minute, waiting for a policeman behind a bullet-proof glass to buzz me in, before I am aware of what I am doing, and then scramble to put my own key in my own lock. Maybe she would never meet someone whose man is doing ten years or fifteen and think, *Wow, that's all? They're lucky.* I have thought that. I have thought that more than once.

And maybe she would never look down at her her wrists, as I have looked down at my wrists, and thought she saw red welts on them, as though it had been her, not him, who had been yanked out of a car, thrown down on the concrete, legs kicked open, arms pulled almost out of their sockets, hands cuffed extra-tight behind her back. Maybe she would never have to say out loud to herself, as I have had to say out loud to myself, that it was he not she who did the crime. It was he not she who was in prison, that all she had ever been guilty of was loving someone.

I looked back over at Elisabeth and for a moment I wanted to say all of these things. I wanted to warn her because no one had warned me, and somebody should have. Somebody should have sat me down and said how their life became. They should have shown me their before and after pictures, but no one did, and I wanted to prepare this young girl, and at one point I even took a deep breath. I took the kind of breath you take just before you lapse into a difficult monologue, but the minibus pulled into the first prison complex where she had to get off but I had to stay on, because I don't get off until the third and final complex in that poor, broken-down, winding fifteen-mile region of prisons. She had to leave right then, and so all I said was, *Have a great visit!*

And later, in the afternoon, when our visits were over and we were sad and exhausted and falling into and out of sleep, it seemed out of place. It seemed like it would have been salt in the wound to say, *This is just the beginning. You're about to feel like this for a very long time. You're about to feel even worse than you do right now. More lonely. More isolated.* In the hours after leaving our partners, I feel like we should have the right to honor silence. We should have the right to hold the last taste of our visits under our tongues. I didn't say a word.

But that night when I was home, I began to feel consumed by the need to talk, to tell what I'd come to know over these years, to tell what I'd seen. I wanted to tell for Elisabeth, but mostly I wanted to tell for me, because it was true what she said, that so many of our family and friends don't understand and so we stop trying to explain, but still there are all these stories in us. Even though so many of us shut down, and become pretenders, and say defensively that *We don't care if nobody knows him because my business is my business.* Even then, we have stories to tell, experiences to share. I have heard so many of them. They get whispered on the vans in the time before and just past the dawn.

They get whispered by the women who, away from the prison, often say to coworkers and acquaintances that they are not married. And by the women who will lie about where they are going every weekend when they hoist themselves and their children and their packages together onto a van before seven in the morning. The stories get whispered by the women who are silent about husbands and lovers at family gatherings. Family gatherings where everybody knows, but nobody says, which is the way it is in my family, and which is why at significant moments in my life, I began to feel like a huge part of myself didn't really exist. Part of me didn't exist because during those times with my family when I should have felt open and unguarded, there was no Rashid. There was no discussion of Rashid, no picture of him, no questions, no arguments, nothing. Rashid had been secreted away as though I was ashamed of him. I am not ashamed of him. I thought about that the night after the day when I met Elisabeth.

And I thought about how, when Elisabeth spoke of her sense of isolation, it underscored my own sense of isolation, and it would have been so easy right then to disappear into the pain, into the insanity, of prisons. And I couldn't let that happen. After all these years I knew I owed myself and I owed Rashid and I owed our relationship more than disappearing. In the very least, even if from that day forward, I never went up into a prison again, if I never saw Rashid again, I owed us the truth. The whole, entire, out-loud, in-public truth, which meant I had to admit that despite all of the losses and all of the hurt, there were these moments in Rashid's arms that were a luxury of bliss. There were these times when we shared an absolute embarrassment of love. There were days that had set a standard for days.

And because of those moments and days, I knew that I also owed to us to proclaim as loudly as I'd cried after we lost the appeal, after everything that had ever cut me or cut Rashid these last seven years, that at the end of the twentieth century, when there were some people who, more than anything else, wanted the stock market to keep booming, and some who wanted to lose another fifteen pounds, and some who wanted to become big stars in small films, and some who wanted brand-new sports utility vehicles, and some who wanted Clinton impeached, and some who wanted to rock Hilfiger gear daily, and some who wanted to write rhymes and make phat beats, and some who wanted their next ten-dollar bag of whatever they could sniff or shoot or smoke away, and in a time when most of us wanted cures for AIDS and cancer and a realistic way to keep our blood pressure down, the greatest of my own personal needs was for my husband to come home to me.

To come home to me healthy and to come home whole, right then, in the very second that I was wishing for it. I realized that I wanted Rashid home more than I wanted to write the next line or poem, and more than I wanted to run the next mile, because at the core of me I felt certain I could always write and I could always run, but what I could not do was beg or borrow or broker or bribe back time. And to my great surprise, this realization did not plunge me into a greater sadness. It did not make me think about all that I was missing. It made me think about all that I had. It made me think I was blessed. To want someone like that. To be wanted by someone like that.

And in my room that night, sitting cross-legged on my bed, watching the first coat of night drape over the trees and garage outside my window, I began to smile and I began to cry, because all at once I could remember how full I felt when I did no more than hold Rashid's hand, and I could also remember how nullified I felt when I had to leave. But those memories weren't what was important. What was important was that while I was going up and back over good memories and bad ones, I did not feel alone, although surely I was alone in that room. It did not matter. For the very first time, I did not feel it to be so. I felt Rashid was right there, beside me. I could not see him, but I could smell the oil he wears. It was there, that particular scent, on the inside of my hands. And I could imagine his touch. I closed my eyes. My flesh reacted. It twitched. It went flush, and when the heat eased, I opened my eyes and reached for my journal and waited.

I waited for my emotions to transform themselves into language, into something that would remind me and Rashid in our very worst and most difficult times, when we are in some visiting room thinking that all there is to see are the towers and the guns and the razor wires that circle everywhere above us like vultures arrived too soon, that we are alive. Despite how much harder the bid has gotten since Rashid lost the appeal. Despite all the anger and anguish and quivering faith and rushing confusion, we are alive and somehow together. And we might not have been.

There might have been another story to tell, for Rashid and for me, and it might have been a horror story and it might have been a tragic story, and mostly it might have been a separate story. Rashid's in one book, mine in another. But the story we have written, the one which is bigger and more defining than all the other stories, was the one which would begin with the words I finally wrote late that night. I wrote five words over and over that two years later became this book, but when I started, the only thing I could think to say, the only thing I thought I needed to say, was that this is a love story. That's what I wrote, all down one page and then down another. This is a love story. This is a love story.

28 July

Beloved,

Here is the base of night where I can meet you. I can always meet you, here, where the day has ended, and the dark has come like a reverent lover, to carry me back to myself, to give me back to my prayers. I meet you here in silence every night of my life, Rashid. Have I told you this before? I know I'm not supposed to write you a letter like this.

I said I wouldn't write you a letter like this, given the state of things between us. Yesterday I read a card that you gave me once at the end of a trailer visit. The card said sometimes it's good to leave, to wrap yourself in the cloak of quiet, to sit alone, to reacquaint yourself with your dreams. Of course you are my dreams and of course the prison is my nightmare. How do I separate the two, Rashid? When we began you said you were sure I would get used to things, that with time, the pain would become more manageable. It never did.

I have to confess something to you, beloved. I am praying that you will call me tonight. I know I was the one who said we should limit our contact but I am praying each time the phone rings that it's you. I want you to call me tonight, and I also wanted you to call me last night, and I also wanted you to call me the night before that. You have always asked of me this one thing: to make a decision and to stick to it. I'm trying to, Rashid. I know I said I needed some time away, and I remember how I struggled to get you to understand, and I know I'm not doing very well. Have I said yet that I love you? Have I said how loving you keeps complicating the picture, obscuring my escape route out of this prison life?

Sometimes I wonder if you know how much I think about you. I could spend every hour of every day lost in the memories *of how we are together. Maybe that's why I wrote this book. So I could legitimize daydreaming about us being together. Remember the last time we were on a trailer and I asked, Can I look at you, Rashid? Before we make love, I asked, can you step back and can I look at you? And you said yes and took off everything, and stood there before me and let my fingers trace your scars and veins and sinew.*

You are the most beautiful man I have ever seen. You are the most beautiful man I could ever hope to see. Did I say that then? That your beauty overwhelms me. It distracts me. Sometimes I have to look away from you in order to talk to you, and sometimes I have to forget what you look like, and sometimes I have to forget everything. Sometimes I have to leave everything we are and have been in a closet, all packed up and hidden, so that I can move from one hour into the next.

Memory can be such a tease, a stripper disappearing behind the fast dark curtain with a smile. You can look but you can't touch. What happens when you need to touch and there's only the air and the air is hot and tight and does not serve you?

Last night when it was late, I took a taxi home. The name on the driver's license was the same as your family name, and as we bumped through the streets of Manhattan, and over the Brooklyn Bridge, and up Atlantic and then Washington Avenues, I fantasized that the driver was you and that we had a conversation that started out about politics but ended up with us falling in love. Only this time you came home with me. You came home with me right then in the very moment we fell in love. This time no walls, no police, no doors without keys, no vans, no visiting rooms, no dress codes, no state-issue green pants, no kissing on the clock, no stolen touches, no loneliness, no leaving. Maybe it was a silly thing to do, but hunger breeds a strange appetite, and besides it made the ride go quickly.

You keep asking, How can I go away from you? I never know what to say when you ask. I could never really leave you, Rashid. I just can't face the prison anymore. That's not true. I can face the prison. What I can't face is turning my back another time and walking alone, out of that door, looking once over my shoulder to see if you are watching me. You always are.

Anyway, the truth is that I don't believe this separation will be forever. I can stay away now because I look into tomorrow and see you there. I see the sky seduce its own self with its own colors and then turn into a sweet, thick dusk with stars galloping in the background. That's where you are, in the starbright distance walking toward me, smiling the way you always manage to smile, even when everything inside you feels like it's being quartered, and then quartered once more. I know you felt this way the last time we saw each other. I swear it took all the courage I had to look past your brave front. I didn't want to see how much I was hurting you. I wanted so much to believe that you were really doing fine, but we have never lied to each other. I had to look.

Rashid, I want you to know something I did not tell you the last time we saw each other when I said that I had no idea how I was going to make it through the next three hours on the visit, let alone the next five years on the bid. You looked at me so soberly I could feel myself tremble. You asked, What do you want me to do, asha? Tell me and I'll do it. Do you want me to figure out some way to be up out of here?

And when you said that, my heart skipped. I began to panic, and I almost screamed No! No! I said they would kill you, and you, in the same sober voice, said, Listen to me, asha. If I am killed trying to get to you, it would be the most noble death I could die. Do you remember that?

And do you remember how afterwards I was so quiet? For the rest of the visit, I was so quiet and I just stared at you. I know you wondered why and I know I didn't explain. I couldn't. I was an incomprehensible maze of emotion then. But if I could have, I would have told you how much I wanted to be noble for you too. I would have said that you deserve that. You deserve that from me. And if I had had it in me to speak that day I would have told you that in some small way, this book I have written about us has been my attempt at being noble.

I have never told you how terrified I am of taking our love and placing it out on a public dais to be viewed and scrutinized, but Audre Lorde said if we could learn to work when we were tired, then we could learn to work when we were afraid. And when I thought about that, I wondered, What if you are tired and afraid at the same time? I've been tired and afraid at the same time, but I realize that you have been too, and so I figured if you could keep loving me then in the complete way you've been loving me, then I could keep writing with the same vigor. That was the bottom line, and that was how I wrote every single word I wrote. That was how I wrote even when the memory that those words contained nearly broke me down. That's how I did it.

I have so much work to finish right now, but I don't want to stop writing you this letter. I wish we were talking, that you were here in front of me, but I would even settle for the phone. Did I tell you that I've been praying you would call me tonight, and that I prayed the same thing last night, and the same thing the night before that? I miss your voice so badly. I *keep trying to hear it in my head, like a favorite song or great speech, but all I hear are snatches. I can't hear the whole verse, never a whole quote. My God, I miss your voice. I miss everything about you. I miss the way you nod your head when you're listening to me. You have always made me feel brilliant.*

I miss the way you can look like a seven-year-old boy and a big grown man all in the same instant. I miss the way you look at me when you want me. I miss your hunger. I miss your passion for life and for justice and for young people and for Islam. And for me. I miss your passion for me. I miss that most of all. It's what I always wanted. It's what I never had. Until you. I miss you. In my eyes, in my ears, on my skin, on my legs, on my stomach, and face. I miss you in my mouth, behind my teeth, under my tongue, on the very tips of my fingers. My hands have become less useful, not touching you.

You might think this is, Rashid, but this is not a good-bye letter. I'm just writing down my heart for you so you can always go back to it and know how I feel. Isn't there a song that goes: Don't say good-bye, always say see you later? I do not say good-bye in this letter, because good-bye is meaningless between people who have loved each other with all the clarity and precision with which we have loved each other. I do not say good-bye, Rashid. I just say see you in a minute, baby. See you in a minute.

The Prisoner's Wife
A Memoir

asha bandele

A Readers Club Guide

ABOUT THIS GUIDE

The suggested questions are intended to help your reading group find new and interesting angles and topics for discussion for asha bandele's *The Prisoner's Wife*. We hope that these ideas will enrich your conversation and increase your enjoyment of the book.

Many fine books from Washington Square Press feature Readers Club Guides. For a complete listing, or to read the Guides online, visit

http://www.simonsays.com/reading/guides

A conversation with asha bandele

Q: You've spoken elsewhere about the idea of "writing yourself into existence." What do you mean by this?

A: When I think about this statement, I think about what it means to be part of a group of people whose story has historically been distorted when it was not, as Audre Lorde said, completely erased. I am committed to the idea that I, as a Black woman and writer, have a right and responsibility to insert my/our story, as honestly as possible, into a public dialogue. My work should challenge the stereotypes, add dimension, complicate the picture of who I/we are in the world.

Q: With *The Prisoner's Wife*, you've not only written yourself into existence; you've given voice to an entire population of prisoners' wives, who are all too often an afterthought when it comes to criminal justice policy and practice. What sorts of feedback have you received?

A: The majority of people have been very supportive. Other wives have e-mailed and written me to say that they felt that I wrote a book that emotionally reflected their lives. Of course not everybody loved it. Some have said that they had a better, more powerful love story to tell, and they didn't feel I truly showed how Rashid and I were in love. They said I took a lot for granted. For example, when I complained about the way conjugal visits were handled, some women said... "well I don't even get conjugal visits, so asha should just be happy." But I've never been a person who found it useful to say that at least I wasn't forced to live under the worst conditions. I think it's much more useful to look at what should exist and struggle for that. In any case, the general opinion I was made privy to was very supportive.

Q: How, and at what age, did you begin writing poetry? Did your parents play a role in your aspirations?

A: I've been writing poems since I was about 8 years old. I've been writing in a serious and focused manner, though, since I was in my late teens.

Q: Did you show your manuscript to Rashid or any other loved ones before publication? Did you feel any anxiety in the time leading up to *The Prisoner's Wife's* release?

A: No one is more supportive of my writing than Rashid, and so, yes. He saw the manuscript in its many incarnations prior to publication. In fact, I read nearly every chapter to him over the phone and he listened and commented on how it impacted him, positively or adversely.

As far as having anxiety prior to publication, I had a great deal of it. I thought that there would be a nasty right-wing backlash—and to a very small degree there was. But for whatever reason, it didn't hurt me. Even when people called me crazy or made other insulting remarks about my character, I felt that they did not know/understand me or my relationship. I felt that they came to the page with a lot of preconceived notions. Maybe this is true, maybe it's not, but this belief allowed me to stand before audiences across this country and tell the story even when I felt afraid.

The worst anxiety I felt was how my parents would react to the book, but they've just been supportive of me, even when the decisions I've made are not decisions that they would have made for me. Their willingness to stand with me alleviated my worries.

Q: *The Prisoner's Wife* has come out in the midst of a so-called "memoir explosion" in publishing. What is it about a well-written memoir or autobiography that many of us find so much more engaging than a novel or biography?

A: I think that the best memoirs, because they concern themselves with people who are walking and breathing beside us, have the ability to make us feel less alone, perhaps less crazy, more connected. This is particularly urgent in a time when our technological reality separates us from one another more and more. Humans are essentially beings who need companionship, and I think a good memoir can provide that. The protagonist can almost feel like a friend. Many of the people who wrote to me after the book came out said that they felt like they knew me forever, that we were somehow friends although we'd never met.

Q: Do you feel an affinity with other memoir writers working today?

A: I feel an affinity with other writers in general. Anyone who writes a story that helps to further illuminate the world for me gives me a sense of validation. I was though, I should say, encouraged by the bravery of many memoirists—Kathryn Harrison comes to mind immediately. I felt if those writers could summon the courage to tell their story, why couldn't I tell mine?

Q: You invoke the words of fellow poet and memoirist Audre Lorde in this book, as well as the music of Nina Simone—whose powerhouse version of Bob Dylan's "I Shall Be Released" speaks directly to your book's themes. How have these women influenced your work?

A: Audre Lorde had a profound impact on me as a writer and as a human being. It was her refusal to give in to silence, lies or denial—even when it seemed safer to do so. This radically changed the way I encounter and engage the world. Nina Simone has an unbridled emotional quality to her work that always carries me to the most intimate place inside of myself. I wanted those qualities to exist in every sentence I wrote: unflinching honesty and bare emotion. No masks.

Q: Which writers and poets do you most admire?

A: I admire and am influenced by the creativity, complexity and truth of Sonia Sanchez, Toni Morrison, F. Scott Fitzgerald, Isabel Allende, Audre Lorde, Dorothy Allison, James Baldwin, Kathryn Harrison, and Edwidge Danticat. I suppose I could list forever. There are so many talented writers available to us. These are the first who come to mind. But I have to also say that different writers have had influence over me at different times in my life. When I first became serious about writing, Audre held a particular urgency because of her messages about breaking silence. I had to hear that message, had to first "transform silence into language" as she said. When I felt comfortable doing that, then I looked to other writers—Sonia Sanchez for example—to see how to tell a poem, a story. Not that Audre was devoid of craft—that's certainly not true, or that Sanchez is somehow devoid of a theory about writing. I'm saying that each writer who influenced me touched me in a particular area that needed examination.

Q: Among artists working in other media—whether film, dance, or music—whom do you feel has most inspired your own work?

A: Again, this question has the possibility of being so expansive that I could never answer it completely, but I can say that the artists who inspire me most are the ones who appear to create fearlessly, without worrying if they'll be loved or hated. Artists who inspire me are artists who take responsibility for the fact that their work has the ability to move people to a higher place of knowing. They do not subscribe to the idea of art for art's sake. When I think about a dancer who fits this description, I think about the late Alvin Ailey. When I think about musicians, I think about Bob Marley and I think about John Coltrane. I think Abbey Lincoln, and I think about Nina Simone. When I think about actors and filmmakers, I think about Julie Dash, Kasi Lemmons, Alfre Woodard and Kimberly Elise. Of course, this is a very, very short list.

Q: One of the most poignant passages of *The Prisoner's Wife* finds you thinking about the welfare of a woman you've never even met: the widow of the man Rashid killed. What do you know about her? Do you wonder whether she has read your book?

A: I don't know anything about her at all—except the one thing that may have changed her life more than anything else. And no, I don't imagine she's ever read the book. This probably, understandably, wouldn't be the book for her.

Q: Yours is the type of writing which flows so organically and musically—moving from page to page so gracefully—that it's hard to imagine it at a stage that's anything less than fully polished. In other words, you make what must be a lot of hard work look easy. Give us the inside scoop on your writing regimen.

A: I don't have a daily regimen per se, but there are things I do because I think they help to make me better at the craft. First of all, I read as much as possible and I read a wide variety of authors. I also read what I write, and I read the work of other authors out loud. It helps me to hear the music and the truth of the language when I do it this way.

I keep a journal, where I don't have to worry if what's in it is quality writing. The journal keeps me engaged with the written word, and allows me to create in an unedited way, which is so important. Sometimes you have to just let it all out, just write and write and write—without an eraser. You can always come back later and clean it up. And that leads me to another point. We have to never be afraid to revise our work, but we also must have the courage to put it down and say, There. All done.

Reading Group Questions and Topics for Discussion

1. In the first passage of *The Prisoner's Wife*, asha bandele powerfully defines the essential nature of her book. Built around five simple words—"this is a love story"—the author unleashes a beautiful litany of similes characterizing the narrative we are about to read. Here, the author tells us, is a story that's as beautiful as "an Alvin Ailey dance," but also one that's "polyester-trying to be pretty, not quite making it." Discuss the various—and often contradictory—ways bandele introduces her story to us. What sort of tone is established in this opening, and how does it color the rest of the memoir?

2. In the particular emotional realm of asha bandele's relationship with Rashid, the challenge of transformation—of fundamental change—is central: prison reform, social reform, and, above all, personal reform. "Of course Rashid needing and wanting to transform was obvious. His history demanded this of him. But I was not without my own issues and they also required examination, their own process of transformation." Discuss how *The Prisoner's Wife* as a whole may be viewed through this lens—as a depiction of personal rebirth, or a pilgrimage toward self-renewal.

3. Plot the key map-points on this journey of transformation. What is bandele's starting point? Rashid's? Where are the two of them at the close of the memoir? What does asha bandele mean when she refers to transformation as an idea that "spiraled inward"? Inward to what destination?

4. bandele tells us that many of her friends "proclaimed I had all power in every part of our relationship. The life or death of our love rested precariously in my hands." In what ways is this true? In what ways false?

5. Other friends of asha see this power relationship in a completely different light, arguing that "Rashid's ability to virtually command me upstate, that my changing the ways of my life in order to allow for prison rules and restrictions, gives him all the power." Discuss how *The Prisoner's Wife* illuminates the complex issues behind the question of prison love and its relationship to power. [How does power, and the various ways it can be exercised, shape the relationships in your own life?]

6. Discuss the ways bandele's love might be seen as something that binds and imprisons her. Then argue the opposite: to what degree does this same love liberate her? Considering this memoir's ambiguous ending, which of these arguments is likely to win out?

7. What roles do the writings and legacies of such women as Angela Davis, Betty Shabazz, Coretta Scott King, and Myrlie Evers-Williams come to play in asha bandele's life? Why does asha feel so strongly at first that she "never wanted to be part of their kind of sisterhood"?

8. How might the revolutionary writings and activism of Angela Davis be seen as an inspirational template for asha bandele? How does Davis's trailblazing work directly inform the themes and challenging questions with which *The Prisoner's Wife* contends?

9. One of the primary engines powering asha bandele's highly praised writing style in this memoir is her complex use of literally hundreds of metaphors. Open the book to almost any page and we find a different metaphor at work, powerfully illuminating the multiple layers of the narrative. On one page, Rashid's absence in asha's everyday life becomes a "renegade boxer," swinging violently at her without rules or referees. On another, the couple's uncontrollable love makes asha feel as if she's "perched at the edge of an airplane," miles above "an unknowable landscape." Discuss the other metaphors bandele employs. Which do you find particularly effective? How does their vividness serve to enrich the book's message?

10. Beyond metaphors, what other aspects of bandele's prose resonate with the music of poetry? Consider how the author's use of rhythm, italics, and imagery help to convey emotion, character, and tension.

11. Although asha bandele's book illuminates one very specific, very unconventional story, her depictions of love and bravery are in many ways universal. In what ways do you identify personally with the themes and issues in *The Prisoner's Wife*?

12. Discuss the rich complexities of asha bandele's exploration of the nature of suffering. Who suffers more as a result of this affair? This is, of course, a question that defies a simple answer—but it is an issue to which asha bandele returns again and again throughout her narrative. What is the author doing here by underscoring the nature of and possibilities behind the act of suffering? What is a prison if not an institution wherein suffering for one's sins is the

central tenet? Does suffering lead to redemption? Can suffering cleanse us? Can it aid in destroying painful barriers? What are the religious undertones going on here?

13. Consider the author's unflinching depictions of alienation, heartache, and love against the odds alongside the works of other writers. How does *The Prisoner's Wife* echo, riff on, and complicate similar themes in such disparate works as Shakespeare's *Romeo and Juliet*, James Baldwin's *Giovanni's Room*, Audre Lorde's *Sister Outsider*, and Wallace Thurman's *Infants of the Spring*?

14. *The Prisoner's Wife* features allusions to *Soledad Brother*, George Jackson's seminal portrait of the struggles, politics, and intricacies of prison life. How has Jackson's book—the work of a brave and embattled black man—influenced our culture's perceptions of political imprisonment, racism, and the United States justice system?

15. In what ways can we view *The Prisoner's Wife*—the work of an equally brave and similarly embattled black woman— as a useful, even indispensable, counterpoint (and complement) to the messages in Jackson's *Soledad Brother*?

16. One of the most striking passages in the book finds asha bandele describing the harsh and omnipresent spotlight of prison guards and surveillance cameras as the "gift that the prison had given" to her and Rashid. What does she mean? How could this possibly be seen as a gift?

17. Chart the ways asha's understanding of and relationship with her childhood evolve over the course of the book.

18. How does the progression of asha's relationship with Rashid influence and run in parallel with her recovery of lost and repressed memories?

19. What do you suppose has happened since asha mailed to Rashid the letter that concludes *The Prisoner's Wife*? What questions do you have for the author?

20. Through your reading of *The Prisoner's Wife*, what were you particularly surprised to discover about the American prison system? Explain how this book might help to challenge or dispel prominent myths and preconceived notions that many of us have about prisoners and their loved ones.

What book will you choose for your next reading group?

Visit

www.SimonSays.com

to keep up on the latest new
releases from Washington Square Press
as well as author appearances, news chats,
special offers and more.

Our WSP Readers Club Guides will help
enrich your reading group discussions by
offering more questions, better and more
focused discussion topics, and exclusive
author interviews.

To help choose your next reading group book
and to browse through our vast library of
available reading group guides, visit us online
at **www.simonsays.com/reading/guides** today.

SIMON & SCHUSTER
A VIACOM COMPANY
www.SimonSays.com

WSP
READERS
CLUB